Pawprints on My Heart

AMANDA JURTA

Pawprints on My Heart
Copyright © 2018 Amanda Jurta

Edited by Brenda Jurta and Marigold Green
Cover Design by Charala
Illustration by Lara Bezich

All rights reserved. This book or any portion thereof may not be reproduced or used in any manner whatsoever without the express written permission of the publisher except for the use of brief quotations in a book review.

First Edition, 2018

ISBN 978-0-9995821-0-7

www.amandajurta.com

*For Mama — I am so blessed to share this journey with you.
And to the canine earth angels who have graced my life —
Thank you!*

CONTENTS

Foreword ix

Chapter One: Renewal 1

Chapter Two: Color My World 15

Chapter Three: Changing Seasons 37

Chapter Four: A New Adventure 47

Chapter Five: The Visitor 75

Chapter Six: Heart and Heartbreak 91

Chapter Seven: Over the Rainbow 115

Chapter Eight: Fresh Eyes 125

Chapter Nine: Home 141

Chapter Ten: Home Again 159

Chapter Eleven: Time Stops 175

Chapter Twelve: Always 195

Afterword 211

Foreword

I had a dream this morning and woke up abruptly to recall the details. We were taking Cocoa somewhere, but it was only a one-way trip. The journey was being shared by many others who faded in and out of the snowy landscape, and now it was just the two of us.

She turned to look at me with those intense eyes, staring at me so I could remember every detail of them. Their round shape, their changing color, and perhaps most impressive, their intent to communicate something far greater than I had the ability to understand at the time. She was sprightly and her brown coat was short, neither a puppy nor fully grown. Her youthful exuberance was welcoming as she bolted forward to lead the way, her strong paws scraping across the icy glaze.

Mama soon joined us and smiled, knowing the company we held. But alas, this one-way trip was on my mind. Why one way? Why were we going to leave Cocoa at the destination? As I beckoned in question, the answer became ever so apparent. This trip would be the tale — the adventure of a lifetime — and I was to tell it from my perspective. And so it begins. My passion is guided, and the story of this incredible dog unfolds.

I'm in the stillness, the quiet,
Then I feel you close.
Hush in the leaf breeze, the green trees...
My heart keys—
Vulnerable.

CHAPTER ONE:
Renewal

I never thought I could love another dog as much as I loved Lady, the beautiful collie who was a gift to our family. I still remember that day when she was placed into my arms, this bundle of white, tan, and black fur, unable to contain her excitement for life. She grew up with us for twelve years, and when her body refused to work any longer and I saw that distant look in her eyes, I just wanted her suffering to end.

Each of us said goodbye to our dear friend under the maple tree in the front yard, her soft coat dampened from our tears. The vet inserted the needle, and the intoxicating chemical smell that coursed through Lady's body overwhelmed my senses. After watching her stare turn to stone, I never wanted to feel that pain of loss again.

A few afternoons had gone by when I was drawn to the window. At the base of the hill where Lady was buried, there stood a lovely doe with her mouth pressed to the ground. For a moment, she raised her head and looked directly at me. I got the distinct feeling that I knew her.

Time seemed to hold its breath as we were locked in this gaze, an unsaid connection occurring until in one fluid motion, she leapt into the woods, her white tail flipping up as if waving farewell. I was in awe of this profound occurrence, and somehow, my grief dissipated. For many nights to follow, there were scratches at the door, but no one was there. Still, I held it wide open and felt strangely comforted, for I believed in more than I could see.

⁓

Our friends had adopted a new dog. Curious to meet her, we found ourselves at their home where Annie, their golden retriever, joyfully greeted us. She used to play with Lady and had a similar gentle nature. I petted her lovingly, tears forming in my eyes as she nuzzled my hand, perhaps picking up on my sadness over our recent loss. She stuck close to us as we made our way to the living room.

"This is Rory!" Gretchen sang out in her energetic teacher voice. There on the floor sat a chubby blond puppy, gnawing on a toy.

"She's adorable!" Katie said. We could feel her delightful energy as she rolled on the floor, fascinated with everything around her. Annie stood nearby and observed her new sister. I brushed my hand along her sweet face until a tug on my shoelaces brought me back to Rory. I giggled.

"It's been so long since we've even *seen* a puppy. She's wonderful—" I laughed as she went for my other shoe. Kathy handed me a book.

"No pressure," she said, "just thought you guys might be interested." The dogs on the cover caught my eye.

⁓

Mama poured a cup of tea and joined us at the kitchen table. Katie shuffled through the coupons while I scanned the rest of the newspaper sections and stumbled upon the Classifieds. A small ad read "Australian shepherd puppies for sale. Canterbury, NH." I grabbed the dog book, rifling through the pages to the picture and information about the breed, and held it up.

"It won't hurt to go and *see* them!" I smiled. We were all in agreement.

"I'll bring money just in case," Mama said with a newfound cheer. We piled into the jeep and headed out to meet the advertised puppies. I couldn't ignore the excitement I felt.

⇀

We arrived at the house, and a middle-aged woman with a dour expression on her face walked toward us. As Mama spoke with her, an unmissable ball of brown fluff came tumbling along in the tall grass. I was in love. "She's the last one," I heard the woman say. "I don't have papers for her. My daughter drove her here from out west." Papers schmapers. This pup was ours.

Katie and I already agreed on her name, which her warm chocolate appearance begged for. "Hi, Cocoa!" I said, picking a blade of grass and twirling it to attract her attention. She bounded at my hand, grabbing it in her tiny teeth and falling down to reveal a chubby, pink tummy with caramel-blotched pigmentation. She was asking to be tickled. A tuft of white hair marked her chin, and standing out against her short brown coat was a bib of white. Her little tail, a two-inch stub, seemed to have a mind of its own as it whirled around.

A fit of barking from the side of the house stole me from the moment, and as Katie played with Cocoa, I wandered over to see what the commotion was. I expected to see a dog, but was shocked when I saw too many of them to count in a small fenced area at the back of the house, full of scrap junk and tall weeds. None of them looked very happy or friendly. I had a sick feeling in my stomach. We were undoubtedly rescuing an innocent puppy from this dark and mysterious place.

Safe in the jeep on the way home, we couldn't get enough of Cocoa. She was so soft, her pads felt like delicate flower petals tapping across our laps, and her energy only increased during the ride. We were about to find out how opening our hearts once again was a way to honor Lady and help us heal. *Love* was the answer.

I hoped Cocoa would like her new home in the rustic, wild surroundings. It didn't take long to see that she did as she happily explored the earthen matter and anything that moved. She frolicked around the yard and we chased her, letting her tackle us until she got stuck in Katie's long hair.

She found the cool slab underneath the woodstove and was just small enough to fit there, the height of a piece of wood, and opened her mouth into a wide yawn, her tongue curling at the tip. I watched her eyelids droop, and she dozed into a deep slumber. She had only been in my life for a few days, yet this brown bundle of fur had already captured my heart.

The house was full with puppy energy, and I couldn't wait to get home from my summer job to see Cocoa. We'd play and play, but her social behavior during the day changed at bedtime when she chose to be as far away from everyone as possible. The first night she disappeared. Mama and Katie hadn't seen her, and neither had let her outside.

We searched the house until finally, I knelt to look under the couch and found her stretched far back against the wall, completely unreachable. "Cocoa, come here." I tried coaxing her toward me, but she wouldn't budge. I started to wonder what she went through in those early weeks at that woman's house. She must have been afraid.

But after introducing her to the window view from my bed, where fresh air flowed in and the front yard activities were visible, she fell asleep there, dwarfed amongst my stuffed animals. I awoke to her skunky puppy breath on my face in the middle of the night. She licked my nose before rolling over, her puffy belly facing the ceiling, and I rubbed it until she was sleeping again.

Her high-pitched bark announced the morning as she peered out the window. I put my face next to hers to see Mama feeding the birds. "Hi, Mama!" I called. She looked up at us with a smile.

"Hi, Amandy! Hi, Cocoa!" she said, scrunching her fingers in her trademark wave. "How did you sleep?"

"Not bad. She only woke up once." Cocoa pawed at a fly on the screen. "We'll be down soon!" I sat up in bed and wiggled my toes under the sheet. Cocoa was intrigued and launched herself onto them. I moved. She stopped, stared, waited... I wiggled— ATTACK! She bit at my hair feistily as I picked her up and tiptoed into Katie's room to place her on the bed. She curiously watched the covered body stir, and when my sister's face appeared, she pounced, smothering her with puppy kisses.

Cocoa loved water. This was evident the moment she drank from her large bowl, then stuck her nose in it before splashing out the volume with her paws. It became common to have a drenched floor, but remaining serious when scolding her was difficult. She had this way of scrunching up half her nose in defiance, especially to fingers pointed at her accompanied with the word "no."

It was a hot and humid Saturday, and we lounged outside to catch the intermittent breeze. Cocoa lay in a shady spot chewing on a stick, pausing to study a bug crawling through the grass until her concentration was broken by the deer flies pestering her. She needed some relief, and I had an idea. "What do you think?" I called to Mama, Katie, and Ben as I pulled a pink sled out of the shed. "We can make a little swimming pool for her!"

"Yes!" Katie said. Mama turned on the tap, and my brother sprayed the hose at the sled. Just as the water accumulated, Cocoa tested it one paw at a time and wet her nose, dropping a half-chewed acorn from her mouth. She watched it sink to the bottom before trying to fish it out. I threw in a few more and she seemed to like this, blowing out of her submerged nose to get them. Digging at super speed, she emptied the water and contentedly chewed up the debris. As the sled was filled again, she stepped into it, lapped up some of the water, and plunked down on her belly.

I had another idea. Rummaging through the antique toy box inside, I found a frog bath toy that suctioned water and spat it out. I hustled back to everyone laughing as Katie pulled the sled along while Cocoa jumped in and out of it. Sand, grass, pine needles, pieces of acorn, and fur had gathered in the corners.

Katie dropped the cord, and as if waiting for this, Cocoa picked it up in her mouth, jerking backward to pull it. "Check this out," I said, putting the frog in the sled and submerging him to suction water. I squirted Cocoa, who bit at the water stream, then aimed at Katie.

"Hey!" she cried. I squeezed him and he let out a squeaky sound, a bit like a whimper. He was all out of water. Cocoa was immediately drawn to him and stood watching in suspended animation as I repeated the process, filling up the frog and squirting him in her direction. This time, she grabbed his head with her prickly puppy teeth and shook him from side to side.

We didn't think he had a chance of survival until she dropped him and looked at me. "Hmmm, I wonder what you want," I said through a smirk. The game was repeated, and after an hour of water festivities, the bath frog only lost one webbed toe.

Cocoa played rough with most of her toys, chewing out the eyes, appendages, and internal squeakers, but left the frog unharmed. One night, I sat on the floor with her and dumped out the basket of toys, rummaging through them one by one and giving them voices. Cocoa's little eraser-colored nose scrunched up, and she nipped at Woodstock, Snoopy, and French Fry Guy, all squeaky plastic toys. I bounced Frosty the Snowman on the floor. *"Frosty the Snowman was a jolly, happy soul..."* I sang loudly. Her reaction was one of annoyance as she bit at his head. I moved him just out of her reach and began the song again, then whipped him across the floor for her to chase.

It was altogether different for the frog. "Hey, Legs," I said in a slimy, gruff-sounding voice, hopping him up to Cocoa, who was watching ever so attentively. "How ya doin'? I'm Mr. Froggy!" I squeezed his waterless self, and he let out a whistle in Cocoa's ear. Mama chuckled at my charades.

"Aw," I said in my normal voice, "Mr. Froggy loves you, Cokie!"

"Yeah, Legs," I voiced Mr. Froggy, "I love you. I really do!" Cocoa was besotted by him and whimpered. I took her face in my hands and ruffled her hair before joining Mama for a game of Scrabble. As jazz music played in the background on National Public Radio, some different sounds arose. We looked over to find Cocoa curled up on the floor with Mr. Froggy anchored between her paws, licking him, then whimpering ever so softly. That was the start of her special friendship with that seemingly insignificant bath toy.

The freezer did not go unnoticed. Every time the bottom door was opened and the frost vented out, her little paws thundered toward it. She blocked it from closing, breathing in the cold air she so preferred. We giggled as she tried to lick the ice cube tray, the bag of cranberries on the shelf, and nosed around to see what else was in there. Finished with her investigation, she considered it a good place to nap and rested her small head on the lip of the freezer.

Cocoa quickly learned of what was also accessible to her in the giant cold box. She watched us as we took out things to eat and drink, looking at us for her share. It wasn't long before she would walk to the refrigerator and stare at it, seemingly willing it to open until she realized she needed a human for the job. She looked to whomever was closest and went right on staring until it was opened for her.

⁊

I swayed on the hammock one afternoon, mesmerized by the crown of greenery above until Cocoa broke me from my trance. I put my foot down to still the swing and patted her head. Right when the action stopped, she grabbed the woven rope and pulled it with all her might. The hammock didn't budge, yet she continued with a sense of determination in her successive tugging. I finally surrendered to her cuteness and scooped her up to sit on my belly, pushing off so that we swung together.

⁊

I knew Grampa had to meet Cocoa. I set her on the passenger seat of my car, got in, and fastened my seatbelt. As soon as I turned the key, she hopped onto my lap. "Cokie, we're going for a ride. You have to sit on your own," I tried to tell her, placing her on the seat again. She moved toward me, and I realized it was a losing battle. This was a far cry from the little puppy who once did not want to snuggle near anyone.

During the twenty-minute drive to Grampa's house, Cocoa sat up to peer out the window, her fluffy fur tickling my skin as she turned to watch the scenery. I parked outside the familiar ranch-style house and lifted her into my arms. Music was blaring from inside.

"Hello?" I said, walking onto the breezeway. Cocoa was alert with curiosity. From the kitchen, I could see my grandfather sitting in his big blue recliner at the far end of the living room. "Hi, Grampa!" I walked over to him. "This is Cocoa!" He had a look of surprise and gasped when I placed her on his lap.

His entire face softened while his body seemed to melt into the seat as he held this puppy. He cooed at her, and I knew he was smitten. Cocoa studied him as his large hands gently brushed her coat, sneaking a skunky kiss on his cheek before sliding to the floor. Grampa couldn't take his eyes off her as she explored the living room. I had never experienced a moment like this with a man who was ordinarily so guarded with his emotions.

This was a house where our previous pets were never allowed in, and we had to take off our shoes upon entering, yet Grampa wasn't fazed in the least to have Cocoa traipsing about. I secretly applauded my tendency to push the boundaries for I witnessed something spectacular — Cocoa had unlocked a door to Grampa's heart. From that day on, his visits to see us in the woods increased.

Upon returning home, I was greeted by a very delighted Cocoa. But this time, she was expressing herself in a totally different way, as if her excitement had taken over her whole body. Her walk toward me was more of a shuffle slide as she contorted her middle outward while her bum jittered and swung around wildly. Her little tail bud wiggled frantically, a "love look" radiating from her eyes as she whimpered.

I hugged and praised her, and she dropped to the ground, her mouth agape like a grinning crocodile. Her legs fell open, exposing her blotchy skin, and she let out a low sigh of approval as I rubbed her belly. "I missed you, Cokie," I sang to her. And with that, she got up and bolted for her nearest toy. I chased her as she circled the yard before collapsing on the mossy earth under the staircase.

I could see that Cocoa and I shared an independent nature. We didn't need to be surrounded by others and were quite at ease in our own company. I smiled as I looked out the window to see her lying on the grass, this little puppy casually chewing on a stick without a worry in the world.

I decided to take her for a ride, which led to a spontaneous trip to a "pick-your-own" blueberry farm. After getting a bucket from the farmhand, I drove to a distant section of the field and carried Cocoa to the first aisle. The summer heat was only beginning to taper off, so she readily made her way under a blueberry bush, digging into the cool soil to rest.

And of course, she had already discovered a stick to chew on. "You're such a good girl!" I smiled at her decisive nature, then turned to the plump blueberries. *Plunk!* I dropped the first handful into the bucket, and she looked around to see where the sound came from. "They're just blueberries," I said, offering her a couple from my hand. She sniffed them and gladly licked them up.

As I moved along the row, I kept an eye on Cocoa, who remained in her comfortable spot. Crickets chirped as the afternoon passed, and before long I had picked enough. It was obvious that my little puppy had a taste for the berries as she stuck her face into the brimming pint. I reached in for my share. By the time we got home, they were gone, our blue tongues the evidence of our binge.

As is usually the case with puppies, Cocoa drew attention wherever she went. She was the definition of cute. One morning when Katie and I were on a walk with her, a gold car drove toward us. A window rolled down and a woman's friendly voice oozed compliments for Cocoa. "She's beautiful! What's her breed?"

"This is Cocoa," I said, "she's an Australian shepherd." It was apparent that the woman was captivated by her.

"I'm looking for a puppy, so if you hear of any others, please let me know. My name is Barb, and I live there." She pointed toward her driveway.

"We'll keep our eyes peeled," Katie piped up.

A few nights later, I saw a local ad listing a one-year old "Cocoa" for sale, but her breed was unspecified. I found Barb's house with *my* Cocoa and knocked on the door. No one was there, so I tucked the ad in the window pane. "Well, girl, there might be another 'Cocoa' in these woods soon!" She looked at me inquisitively, then perked her ears when a branch snapped. We continued on our way, through the big open field and onto the pine paths to the pond.

A week or so passed before we got a phone call from Barb. "Thanks for the ad," she said. "I've found a puppy. Come and meet him!" We were excited. Cocoa would have a playmate. She seemed to sense our anticipation and walked with purpose. As we cut through the path at the end of the road, a big dump truck loudly downshifted around the corner, startling her, and she yanked forward.

We crossed the dirt road that led to Barb's driveway. In the distance, I could just make out a little gray and white wolf-looking puppy at her feet. Cocoa noticed him, her tail bud wiggling crazily, and as soon as I unclipped the leash, she took off toward him. One of his ears flopped back as he watched her approach. She stopped right in front of him so they were touching noses until he sprung up and tackled her. All of us laughed.

"This is Suka. He's a husky-shepherd cross," Barb told us.

"He's adorable!" Cheerful puppy barks filled the air as the two became a tangled ball of fur rolling in the grass.

"I think someone's in love," Katie sang. We watched as Cocoa raised her lip in a playful snarl and pawed at Suka's face. Little did we know, we were observing the beginning of a lifelong friendship.

―

Cocoa was growing into her large paws, and our longer walks began. She marched a few paces ahead of me with her exaggerated feminine swing, scoping out new smells and piles of scat. I didn't leash her until we were at the bottom of the road.

One afternoon, I decided to test her. Waiting until she was distracted by a scent trail, I ducked behind the nearest tree, peering around it tactfully to track her. I watched as she put her nose to the ground and snorted into a pile of leaves. Her ears were perked as she gazed downward.

She was entirely focused until she looked up to find me, but I was gone. Jumping off her site of interest, she stared in my direction on the hill and ran toward my hiding place before stopping abruptly. Her concern was clear, and enough was enough. "Rahrrr!" I popped out at her and she barked happily, breaking into a crazy run. "I'm gonna get you!" I cried. From then on, Cocoa kept close, glancing back with a watchful eye on the humans she led.

Suka visited Cocoa almost every day. She knew exactly when he was roaming through the woods and greeted him expectantly. His mission was instinctual at first, marking his spot on the outskirts of the lawn. Once that was accomplished, the two ran all around the yard. Cocoa preferred being chased and tried to entice him by dangling a bone halfway out of her mouth and pushing it toward him. Just when he became interested, she would sprint away, circling the house as long as he was in pursuit.

"Come on, you two! Biscuits!" I called, and they bolted inside. There was a definite rivalry with anything to do with food, mostly on Cocoa's part. Her normally composed behavior with receiving a treat was disregarded as she sat to try and box out her friend, inching forward while looking over her shoulder in protest before turning to me. She was like a snapping turtle, and I had to watch my fingers. I went to give Suka his share. "No, Cokie," I scolded as she nudged in, "he gets one too."

As he tenderly took the biscuit to the hallway, she lunged, causing him to drop it, and gobbled the whole thing down with a satisfied gloat. It didn't take long for Suka to change his habits, so cleverly, Cocoa diverted him away from *her* biscuit jar. She stood at the door, and just when it was opened, she would let him go first, barreling after and causing his hair to stand on end.

Oftentimes, Suka accompanied us to the pond. We cut through Barb's property to pick him up, and the two dogs would gladly meet before the chase began. Cocoa's high-pitched bark signaled her delight until Suka disappeared into the woods. We called it the "wandering male condition." Meanwhile, Cocoa stayed several paces ahead of us, checking frequently to ensure we were still there.

Cocoa followed me toward the raspberry bushes. There were still berries mixed amongst the thorny stems rampantly overtaking them. I leaned way in to reach some plump ones, careful not to get pricked, and soon filled my palm. Cocoa looked at my hand with curiosity, touching her nose to it as I picked through the berries.

"Here you go," I said, finding a big one. She chewed on it while I popped a few into my mouth, their natural sweetness unparalleled by anything I had ever tasted. Cocoa stared at me for more. We sat there together eating wild raspberries in the waning light of the evening as the woods became lively with noise. It was the feeling of simple fulfillment with the being who was easily becoming my best friend.

CHAPTER TWO:

Color My World

It was fall. The temperature was getting to be at Cocoa's comfort level as she flourished outside, no longer panting from simply resting in the heat of summer. The smell of decomposing leaves and spicy earth filled my nostrils, and acorns could be heard dropping in the yard and all around the woods. Cocoa loved acorns.

I sat in the yard and picked one up, rubbed its smooth shell, then casually tossed it near the cabin. Cocoa was suddenly there in front of me, barking excitedly. I picked up another and threw it to her, which she caught in her mouth and chomped down to crack before letting it fall. Her eyes were eager as she backed up with anticipation. I skipped the next one across the ground, trying to get it past her, but she used her front legs to stop it and waited. As I started to hurl them, she moved with amazing agility, preventing any from getting by her.

I decided to try this game a little differently to test her skills. Along the pine needle paths on the way to the pond, I stopped to gather dried-up pine cones. I caught Cocoa's gaze toward them, and just as I went to pick one up, she pounced on it, crushing it in her powerful jaws with a satisfied look. The remnants fell from her mouth, and she waited for me to find more.

"No, Cokie, they're for later," I said with a grin, waving for her to continue on the paths. There was an abundance of them ahead, and I filled my sweatshirt pocket until it bulged. Cocoa dashed past me, through the pine forest and down the root-laden hill to the pond.

I whistled for her, but I should have known better. She was already inside the boathouse and seemed to predict my plan. I pulled out a pine cone and threw it above her head and across the floorboards. The game began. She tore off, scooped up the rolling object in her mouth, and happily chewed it, quickly discarding the pieces. Turning to me, she was ready and poised for another one. My target was the far wall, but she intercepted. This girl was good.

I emptied my pocket, and she let out a soprano yelp of excitement as the pine cones tumbled onto the floor. Once again she pounced, claiming her next victim. I waved my hand forward before she could go for more. "Back it up, Cokie!" Knowingly, she followed the gesture and waited from a distance, her eyes reading mine.

Each pine cone was kicked in a different direction in effort to "score," but Cocoa stopped every single one of them. All that remained were leftover fragments on the floor. "Okay, girl, switch sides!" I ran around her, and she nipped at my ankles as if herding me. I kicked a piece toward the wall, and there she was, swiftly stopping it. She caught on so quickly that I went through the next pile of debris, switched sides, and repeated.

"Take a break!" I shouted on my way to the boathouse bench. Cocoa raced to the shoreline by the dock and waded in, blowing bubbles through her nose into the water and drinking until her thirst was quenched. Her beautiful hairs fanned outward as she submerged her body and swam in a circle. When she returned to the ramp, her coat was matted down to expose her slender form.

"You're so pretty," I said. She approached the bench and shook, drenching me with pond water. "Cokie!" My saturated shirt clung to me, but I couldn't be upset for long. The culprit gave me a "look" before going into the boathouse and taking position opposite the smithereens, her face tilted in expectation. "Come on, we need more." I stepped through the labyrinth of giant tree roots to find all sorts of prospects, collecting enough that were soft and dry, leaving the spiky green ones for further seasoning.

When I dropped my next handful of pine cones onto our playing ground, Cocoa jumped at them with a joyous bark. "Okay, back it up!" Her eyes met mine before she scooted backward. We played seven rounds, so immersed in the game that time was of no essence. She waded into the water, drank some, blew bubbles, swam, and ran up the ramp, pausing as she started to shake near the bench where I sat. I knew better now and escaped the soaking.

This became our main activity at the boathouse. When it appeared as if we were going to bypass the area, Cocoa would circle, leading me in that direction with begging eyes. The trees dropped more pine cones and our stockpile grew. It was so obvious this game would never lose its appeal.

―

We were constantly coming up with new games for Cocoa. This time, it was a version of Hide and Seek. Using her treats as little incentives, we hid them behind pillows in various locations on the couches. At first, Cocoa chased after me, wanting to eat them immediately. "No, Cokie, you have to wait until I'm done hiding them." I motioned for her to sit until they were in place. Reluctantly, she did. "Okay, go!" She diligently checked every spot, jumping onto the couches and nosing aside the pillows, her eyes wild with an insatiable hunger. Then she double-checked each pillow to ensure none had been missed.

She needed more of a challenge, so we narrowed it down to only a couple of pillows as hiding spots. Cocoa sat, watched, and waited for the go-ahead, then off she went to find them. Every so often she became impatient and wouldn't wait for the game to be set up. An element of trickery had to be added. We raced around faking hides while she trailed us, the pillows strewn all over the living room as she tore through it. One of us distracted her into the kitchen, away from another round of treats being hidden, then the adorably ravenous beast was released for her hunt.

⁓

I was immersed in a book one morning, and a scratch on the front door stole me from my concentration. I could see the tips of Cocoa's fuzzy ears. "Come on in, ears!" I said playfully. She just stood there, a few feet from the door, looking at me. I went to pat her, but she jumped back, evading my hand. "What is it, Cokie?" She turned her head to direct me. I stepped outside and closed the door, and eagerly, she led me around the corner.

Her gaze was toward the exposed cement foundation where I saw a white, half-buried item in a leaf pile. She nudged forward, staring up at me, then back at it until I reached down and scraped aside the leaves to uncover one of her marrow bones. She jumped up excitedly, and I gave it to her. "Good girl! You found your bone! It must have gotten raked into the leaves." I scratched her bum, and merrily, she trailed me to the door but refused to come inside. "Okay, I'm just finishing some reading," I said.

It was only a matter of minutes until there was another scratch on the door. I got up to see Cocoa standing much as she had been before, but now with a very dirty face, her eraser-nose encrusted with soil. "What is it, girl?" She jumped back again, wanting me to follow her. We didn't go far. Her eyes fixated on the empty garden bed next to the rock formation of the outside staircase.

I saw the freshly dug hole with a large mound of shifted soil to the side and swept across the top of it. There was the same white bone. Then it clicked and I understood what was happening — Cocoa was setting up a game of Hide and Seek for *me*. I threw my arms around her. "Oh, Cokie, that was so much fun! Thank you, girl!" She looked at me, quite pleased with herself. I smiled and brushed the dirt from her nose, then kissed it.

Running down the pine needle paths toward Elbow Pond, I felt as free and light as the wind, with my trusty sidekick leading our escape from the busy world. The birds sang gloriously, witnessing girl and dog enjoying nature's bliss. Cocoa waited for my direction, and when I pointed left, she leapt up a sloped hill of dirt. "You're Queen of the Mountain, Cokie!" I shouted, following her up the mound.

She jumped off it, glancing at me briefly, then raced along the grown-in shortcut to Leona's Beach, navigating around saplings, thorns, and poison ivy, and effortlessly jumping over the fallen tree just before the next path. My lungs were thriving in the fresh air as I ran after her, avoiding the exposed tree roots and stopping abruptly to examine some scat. Her soft face inquisitively poked near mine. I used a twig to feel through the pile, breaking it up to reveal strands of animal hair and whole berries, most certainly a product of a coydog.

Cocoa stared at me, and I felt a bratty grin spread across my face. "I'm gonna get you!" I taunted. She bolted down the last leg of the path to the beach and into the pond, blowing bubbles in the water. I tossed a stick past her, and she waded out to retrieve it.

From my rock seat at the shoreline, I watched this beautiful bear-like dog in her element as she paddled through the water. The rough terrain of Ragged Mountain reigned as the backdrop, perfectly mirrored in the water. I was still. My entire body relaxed in this peaceful atmosphere, melting into the sounds of nature, completely unified with all that surrounded me.

Out of habit, I inspected the sand for a flat rock and found one. Just as I skipped it across the placid water, Cocoa let out a shrill cry of delight and splashed toward me, demanding more to be thrown. She shook all over me before nipping at my hands as I hurriedly reached to the ground. "Back it up!" I waved to direct her, but it was useless. She wanted to be up close for this game, and as I attempted to fake a throw, her reflexes anticipated every exact move.

Her yipping echoed around the pond as she frantically ran from side to side chasing falling rocks. "Ten more. That's it, okay, Cokie?" I quickly grabbed another handful, rapidly depleting them as I counted the throws out loud. "All done, girl." I brushed my hands off. "Take a break!" She happily ran back into the water, blowing bubbles once again as she swam. When I turned to leave, she shot by me to circle the rock campfire above the beach, water spraying everywhere as she reclaimed her thick coat. I chased her up the path, catching one last glimpse of the beckoning mountain over my shoulder.

⇀

I knew exactly where to find efts — the cute, orange spotted salamanders that were very special to me. I recalled one dreary afternoon in my childhood when I was unable to avoid the little one crossing our driveway. I had been on my bicycle, coasting down the hill toward the house, when my front tire crushed half of his body. I threw my bike aside and picked up the creature, cradling him in my palm and gently petting his head as tears filled my eyes. I rushed to the house and ran some water into my hand, so desperate to save him, but he no longer moved.

Since then, I vowed to be more observant and move them from harm's way. It was like I became a barometer for efts. With a mild temperature, humidity, and the slightest rain, I knew they would be out. I would find them on the paths in the woods, under fallen branches, in decomposing leaf matter, and especially the ones in harm's way.

Cocoa got her introduction to them one misty day. The orange body meandered toward the center of the path and I reached for it, speaking softly to show I wasn't a threat. Cocoa was immediately interested in what I was talking to, so small to be cupped in my hand. I knelt while she looked at the little creature wiggling in my palm. "This is an eft, Cokie," I told her. "We always protect them." She watched him move around and stared at me as if to register my explanation.

I placed the salamander onto the leafy groundcover off the well-trodden path, and he crawled to earthy freedom. "Goodbye, little guy!" I said, walking a few steps further before spotting a baby one poking his face up. I carefully handled him and studied his pulsating throat, defined eyes, and lined mouth, barely feeling his tiny webbed feet as he crossed my palm and onto my fingers. I moved my other hand closer as he switched direction.

Cocoa ran over to check out the newest acquaintance. Despite our size differences, he must have felt safe for he never peed in my hand. I put him by the first eft and we carried on, consciously keeping an eye out for more of our miniature friends.

I climbed the plank ladder and into the tree house in the pine haven. It was protected amongst the tall trees and densely-wooded section of forest that shielded view of the pond. Cocoa's yellow eyes pleaded to be up high with me, so I carried her to the platform. We sat there together, surveying the area. It was so intensely quiet, as if all of nature was watching itself in this Zen-like moment until it was broken by the single element of a tree creaking in the wind, conducting the chorus of the woods to continue the song.

I lifted Cocoa back down, and we resumed our explorations. As she led the way several paces ahead of me, I ducked behind a tree and waited. Her confident steps stopped, and inconspicuously, I peeked at her. She was scanning the woods thoroughly, waiting for the smallest movement, and I stepped out of sight just before being detected.

"Ooohhhwahhh!" I imitated a bird call to break her concentration and heard her run closer to my position, stopping to search for me. "Ooohhhwahhh!" I repeated, this time a decibel quieter, and snuck my head past the tree to take another look at her. She sniffed the air, and I knew I had given away my location as she honed in on me.

"Rahrrr!" I popped out, and she ran toward me excitedly, dodging my arms to break into a high-speed lap around the trees. Meanwhile, I found a large stick and journeyed onward, dramatically emphasizing each movement until she doubled back to grab the end and tugged it from my hands. Bolting ahead with her wide load, Cocoa ran as I chased her along the sun-streaked undergrowth.

I preferred getting off the road and cutting through the woods whenever possible. One morning as we headed home, I ducked through some branches near the base of the hill. When Cocoa saw me detour, she raced in front to navigate the trail. Just as I rounded the corner by a hardwood tree, the ground softened. I stopped and tested it, lightly bouncing on my feet. It was definitely a weak spot.

A motion caught my eye, and only inches from my shoes popped up a meerkat-looking creature. He didn't seem to notice me as his focus was past my body. He ducked and swayed to the left, then to the right. It was a funny dance until I realized he was actually trying to see around my legs. I pivoted my torso to catch Cocoa staring bashfully at the creature. Then, just as quickly as he had popped up, he departed into the earth.

"Who was that?" I asked Cocoa, her eyes meeting mine until her gaze moved back to the creature who popped up again like a Jack-in-the-box. He repeated his little swaying dance of curiosity before descending once more. Cocoa was calm, and we waited until he popped up a third time, then disappeared for good. "Oh, what a cute little guy, Cokie! He loved you, didn't he?"

We ventured home where I grabbed a wildlife book from the shelf and flipped through the pages until I found a match. "How about that, girl. He's a weasel." She cocked her head sideways at me. "We can call him 'Willy the Weasel!' " On the way home every day to follow, I prompted, "Where's Willy?" and Cocoa immediately understood, running to sniff the ground where he had first popped up, waiting for him to appear again. But he never did.

Sometimes on our walks down the road, we were met by a vehicle driving toward us. Most often, it was family. Cocoa and I were strolling along one day when Katie's jeep came into view. She stopped and jumped out, happy to see us after being away. Cocoa ran to greet her, swaying her bum vigorously.

On another occasion, I was returning from an appointment and could see Mama and Cocoa on the hill. I drove closer and stopped to open my car door. "Cokie!" I squealed out. Alert, she looked in my direction and rushed to me, joyfully wiggling the last few feet before falling into my arms. It was so precious, but we didn't realize what kind of message was being instilled in our young dog by embracing her on the road this way.

One evening, Cocoa walked over to me anxiously. I went to pat her, but she ducked from my reach. "Cokie, what is it?" She stared at the door, and I got up and let her out. A minute passed and she scratched to come in. I knew why she was so antsy. "Do you want to go for a walk?" Her eyes lit up and she raced around in a frenzy. It was settled. "We're going for a quick walk down the road. Back in a bit," I told Mama.

The gravel crunched underfoot, and with dusk setting in, the symphony of night sounds commenced into a hum of varied tones. Cocoa ran ahead to scope out a pile of bear scat on the hill. I could hear a vehicle in the distance, and at that same moment, it occurred to me that she would think someone was coming to see *her*. She took one look at me, her eyes confirming my fear, and started bolting down the road.

"Cokie!" I hollered, my lungs aching as I sprinted after her as fast as I could. "Wait!" It was useless. I was about twenty feet from her when the jeep rounded the corner of the next road. She stopped in the middle of it, the headlights illuminating her body as the vehicle approached. I was just too far away and watched helplessly. "STOP! STOP!" I screamed, frantically waving my arms. My breath was in my throat, and as if in slow motion, the vehicle stopped — *three feet from Cocoa*. She casually glanced at the jeep before jumping onto the embankment past the road. I signaled to the driver with relief.

Grabbing Cocoa's collar, I hugged her face to mine. "Oh, you scared me so much! I thought you were going to be hit!

Never do that again, Cokie! Come on, we're going home." She didn't protest and walked alongside me. I was suddenly aware that my whole body was shaking. Every walk thereafter, I made sure she was leashed well before the road intersection. I only had to learn that lesson once, and thankfully, it was a best-case scenario.

I reflected on my travel through the Australian outback after graduating from college. My friend Silke and I had just visited the iconic Uluru, "Ayers Rock." We stopped at a dusty service station for fuel, and when we went to pay for it, a little sign posted on a bulletin board caught my eye. "Singing Dog Performance. Tonight @ 6 p.m." I was mystified. A singing dog? Sounds intriguing, but how? The idea stayed with me. Two years later, I sat facing the piano at home.

Cocoa had followed me upstairs to rest on the cool floorboards. I started dabbling on the keys and she whimpered. I paused to look at her. "Are you okay?" She stared at me, seemingly fine. Back at the piano, I played a chord. She whimpered again, but I played on. Her whimper turned into a yawn as she opened her mouth and howled the same sounds. It was beautiful.

As I continued to play, she stood up. "Yay, Cokie!" I switched to an old song I knew by heart and watched her as my fingers hit the keys. She was fully belting out notes, holding them after four or five, and that's when I realized — *Cocoa is a singing dog!* She walked around the living room, crooning along with soul, her entire body engaged in delivering this solo performance. I was filled with amazement and pure happiness for sharing yet another passion with my best friend.

The sun streamed through my window and radiated its light around the room, stretching to the walls, then whisking through Cocoa's hair. The diffused glow from the solar glass was a warm awakening as a calm, early morning breeze whispered past the screen. It was a perfect mountain day. I looked at Cocoa and her eyelids popped open, her eyes wide as if she knew. "Wanna go for a hike?"

She let out a little whimper and jumped onto the floor, pacing the living room in expectation. I quickly tied on a bandana, changed clothes, and grabbed a backpack. "Morning, Mama," I sang out as I skipped down the stairs after my pup.

"Morning, Amandy," Mama answered from behind a book and a big cup of tea. She put the book aside to ruffle Cocoa's hair. "Morning, little Miss Cokie Bear."

"Thought we'd go for a hike," I said. Mama peered out the window.

"It seems fine now, but I heard it's supposed to storm."

"Oh well, we should be okay." I ate a banana while Mama fed Cocoa.

"Making your usual," she commented as I put together a traditional Fluffernutter to eat on the summit.

"Mmmm, it's so yummy." I wrapped the sandwich in tin foil and packed it with a couple of water bottles and a bowl. "We won't be too long." Our fastest time up the mountain was twenty minutes. Cocoa looked at me eagerly as I swung the backpack over one shoulder and went to the door.

"Have a good hike!" Mama's cheerful voice called.

"Thanks. If we're not home in four hours, send out a search party!" I joked.

Cocoa was already poised with her front paws on the center console and hind legs on the back seat. I leaned my head to rest on hers. She knew exactly where we were in relation to the mountain, and the moment I indicated the left turn onto the connecting road, she started whimpering. The windows were down low and as the fresh air flowed in, she hung her face out to meet it.

A quarter of a mile from the trail base, she couldn't contain her excitement. Her whimper erupted into a shrill shriek that made my ears ring. "Cokie, we're almost there!" I needlessly reassured her. She hopped into the passenger seat and stuck her nose out the window, barking at the increasingly dense woods before the toll station. When I stopped to pay the state park fee, her tone changed and she was now my skeptical protector. Her shriek became gruff as she told the park attendant that his presence wasn't welcome. With a quick greeting, I handed the dollar bills through my partially opened window.

"Do you need a map?" he asked.

"No, thank you," I managed to say between Cocoa's barks. "We know this mountain well!" I waved and proceeded to the near vacant parking lot. "Hopefully, we don't run into anyone." I turned to my excited little brownie. It was really special to feel like we were solo explorers of the mountain.

I reluctantly leashed her on the way to the trails. It was our custom to take the steepest one on the ascent and return via the longer, more gradual decline. Cocoa investigated the area as we headed to the first trail. "Okay, girl!" The coast was clear, so I freed her. She raced off and doubled back, picking up a scent in the deeply refreshing air before resuming her lead.

I stopped to take a photo of her on the rocks. She was meant for the mountains. She had such confidence since her first hike as a young dog, and each tree root, cavern, rock, and mountain stream was memorized. Nature dominated with musky earth smells, bird calls, and tall pines creaking in the forest, seemingly acknowledging us as we passed. Cocoa kept a comfortable distance between us, and I knew she was "Queen of the Mountain" and the mission as she continually checked on me.

Another familiar bend, and there was our meditation rock. I gave Cocoa some water and we sat together in the stillness of the morning, soon becoming noisy with sounds of fluttering wings and things dropping from the canopy of leaves above. A chipmunk scurried around behind us, undisturbed by our presence. We were at peace, absorbing the surroundings in silent communication.

Cocoa finally looked at me, keen to move on. The steepest part was ahead, an obstacle course like second nature to navigate. A mountain stream gushed across the trail, and she maneuvered over the jagged rocks and dipped into the water, blowing bubbles before lapping it up. I held my hand into the flow and watched it pass through my fingers, cold and invigorating, cleansing my skin.

I was mesmerized until Cocoa raced past me in hyper-mode, her body five sizes smaller as her wet coat clung to her. We ran to the clearing amidst the evergreen forest carpeted with pine needles, stopping to take in its beauty and the strong scents that filled the air. I observed her in the presence of all this — youthful and without boundary. Her ears perked up, readily interpreting the environment, and I only wished I could hear everything she could.

She led me through the next rocky section and up a steep shortcut to the first scenic viewpoint. The wind was strong as I climbed onto the sloped boulder, so I sat to ground myself. Cocoa drank from a small pool of water collected in a triangular cavity in the rock, then quietly surveyed the territory with me. Staring out at the vast land, distant mountains, thick forests, and blue lakes, it made me further appreciate being raised in the countryside. There was so much to admire, to explore… It was liberating.

Cocoa jumped off the rocks to resume the ascent, carelessly wading through the muddy water I sidestepped. Cairns marked the way toward the summit, and a couple walked in our direction as we approached the lookout tower. Cocoa growled and I rushed to hold her while they passed. At the metal wall beside the tower, I searched for something sharp to carve the date of our hike, then stopped to examine the multiple times we had experienced this mountain. I smiled. We just kept coming back.

A low growl once again told me we should move on as another couple arrived. Cocoa really acted like she was Queen of the Mountain. "This way, girl!" I called, finding the steeper route to our usual viewing spot at the eastern side of the mountain. I reached into my backpack and took out the foil-wrapped sandwich. "Fluffernutter, Cokie!" She was at my hands, hungrily gobbling pieces with oozing peanut butter. I hurried to eat my half before feeling obligated to share it with my famished companion.

My sweat dried quickly as I followed Cocoa's gaze into the breezy horizon. I smoothed her coat and readjusted her harness. She turned to look at me, irritated with the restriction. As I sat there letting my mind slip from thought, she wandered the area, guarding the site we had chosen. Her mouth hung open as she panted, her eyes and ears alert, her soft colors highlighted by the morning glow.

On the descent, I caught her before she waded into an alpine bog. Mud splattered onto my legs as I tried to avoid puddles, but not Cocoa. She lay in each one, immersing herself and blowing bubbles in the water, her coat grimy and covered with leaf debris. At lightning speed, she darted around obstacles without a single collision. It was like this all the way down the mountain. I couldn't stop laughing, giddy with adrenaline, feeling weightless and wild.

"Cokie, take a break!" I called out breathlessly. We stood amongst some birch trees, their yellow leaves so magnificent I had to take a photo. A woodpecker hammered away in the distance. Cocoa looked at me with a defiant eye, then went running toward the voices near the end of the trail. I struggled to keep up with her.

I could see people with a black lab, and luckily, Cocoa was distracted by their dog and didn't growl at them. I leashed my boisterous sidekick, and we lingered in the mountain ambience. What an exhilarating excursion it had been with my Cocoa Bear. "You're the best hiking buddy," I said on the drive home, glancing over my shoulder to find her fast asleep on the back seat.

Mama sat across from me at the kitchen table while Cocoa was sprawled out on the floor between our feet, her chin resting on the rail of the chair as she faced the door. She was a growing girl, not quite a year old. Her eyes changed from their puppy turquoise to a pale yellow with tawny flecks, a ring of turquoise remaining on the border of her irises. Her coat was luxuriant and had deepened into an auburn color, wispy feather-soft hair grew behind her ears, and blond pantaloons hid the tops of her legs. She was filling out, muscular and strong.

It was time for an afternoon snack. Mama got out some vegetables, crackers, and cheese. I felt Cocoa shift. As I chewed a peanut butter celery stick, there was weight on my knee. I peered at the unmistakable source. The little tuft of white hair at the tip of her chin was angled upward, her eyes inquiring. I traced along her nose with the side of my finger. "You gorgeous girl," I said, then returned to my snack. She nudged me, resting her chin a little harder on my leg. *Hint hint.*

"Okay…" I put the base of a carrot in my mouth, holding it tightly, prompting her to grab the end. I let go to send her chomping away. Next, I held a cracker in my mouth. Mama gave me a look. Cocoa's eager face moved closer to mine as I leaned down to feed her. She rushed toward me, but I moved back before she could make contact. "Uh uh," I shook my head.

When I repeated the move, she had a calmer approach and took the cracker from my mouth, her wet nose touching mine. I giggled. "Good girl." I bit into another carrot and her chin was on my leg again. I grinned and reached for a piece of cheese.

"Amandy," Mama said as she watched me put half of it into my mouth, "don't do that! You're like a mother bird feeding her young!"

"But she's so cute," I managed to say through the cheese. She rolled her eyes at me as I defiantly turned to the expectant pup.

This began my history of feeding Cocoa from my mouth. It was all about building trust and teamwork through nonverbal communication. Cocoa picked up on it quickly. I fed her increasingly smaller pieces, and she became gently precise in taking them, never once nipping me. Soon I could just nudge my chin in the air and she would mimic me, knowing that she would get something to eat in return.

⇁

Bubbles. When she learned what these were, a mere utterance of the word would send Cocoa into a ripple of anticipation. I found this out one day when I discovered a bottle of them on top of the dresser downstairs. "BUBBLES!" I shouted to Cocoa and opened the cap, blowing through the dipper, sending them floating across the room. At first, she watched as they fell to the floor and popped, but only a few minutes later, she was jumping high to break them midair. I put the bottle away and waited. "BUBBLES!" I repeated. Cocoa started bouncing on her hind legs as I reached for them.

"Buh, buh, buh—" Her barking changed to a high-pitched squeal as the soap circles drifted toward her, and she quickly ended their brief existence. "Okay, little brownie, back it up." If I wasn't careful, my legs would be covered in scratches as she sprung up every time I raised the dipper. After this brief introduction, I took the bottle outside. Her excited barks ricocheted off the trees, notifying the entire forest of her happiness.

Cocoa had grown to be quite protective, and bubbles became a handy tool to bribe her inside when we heard someone driving up the road. She didn't trust any "outsider" men and was cautious around any "outsider" women. Her trust was to be earned. The person who would check the electricity meter, the UPS delivery guy, the propane gas man, and even Grampa. She was clear on her boundaries. And she especially didn't like it if they were wearing anything to mask themselves, be it sunglasses, a hat, or a hoodie.

For as many times as we were able to distract Cocoa before a suspected intruder arrived, the bubbles trick proved to be just another short-lived lure. One morning, I heard a vehicle barreling up the road. Cocoa's bark from the front yard told me I was too late as I ran to the door to call her in. I couldn't see her from the window, so I stepped outside and spotted a truck. Cocoa stood fifteen feet from it.

A tall, thin man looked at her warily. She heard me behind her but refused to obey, moving closer to the stranger. "I'm here to read the meter," he said, which was only a few yards from where he had parked. Bravely, he walked toward it.

"Cocoa, buh, buh, buh—" I tried to entice her with the promise of her new favorite game, but it was too late. She growled at the trespasser.

"She's guarding you," he told me, slowly heading to his truck.

"You're right," I said, taking several steps backward to distance myself from the situation, hoping this would lessen her degree of protectiveness. But no matter where I was, I couldn't guarantee that she would leave this man alone.

"Okay, I'm going," he said, inching toward his truck door. Cocoa barked at the unfamiliar voice and walked closer to him as he put out his hands.

"Cocoa!" I called in a different tone. She turned, giving the man enough time to find the door handle and jump to safety. "Sorry about that!" I shouted. He waved and sped away, happy to put as much distance between us as possible. Cocoa chased him halfway up the driveway with a couple more disapproving barks, then acknowledged me. "Buh, buh, buh—" I ran to the house and she bolted past me, yipping with delight. The "BEWARE OF DOG" sign was put at the top of the road after that.

We weren't receptive to another stranger until he was in the front yard and Cocoa's ferocious-sounding bark rang out. Unbeknownst to me, the UPS man in the brown truck was a well-seasoned professional when it came to coping with protective dogs. "Bubbles, Cokie!" I shouted from my bedroom window. She paused momentarily to look up at me before turning back to the man. I watched as Mama went out to collect the delivery and attempt to shift Cocoa's focus.

As the man handed her a box, Cocoa charged in front of him, but like a magician, he pulled a biscuit from his sleeve and dropped it on the ground for her. Reluctantly, she bent down to pick it up, moving away to eat it, then watched with scrutinizing eyes as he drove off. Although she did not initially like his presence, she came to understand that with the brown truck came a treat. And Cocoa *loved* treats.

There were always a few people who would stop by without prior notice. Cocoa was quick to catch onto those we tried to avoid, her protective tendencies escalating. They would arrive at the most inappropriate hour, when it was past dusk and completely dark. Our vehicles were parked outside, the lights were on in the house, and we were so obviously home, but Katie and I would still hide and wait as the unwanted company knocked on both doors.

Cocoa was sent into a rage when a strange face peered in. Through growls, she stared toward our hiding spots to protest her containment, but we remained quiet, briefly trapped in our own house. When the visitor finally gave up and drove away, we broke into laughter, relieved to escape another confrontation.

Fall transitioned to winter and Katie moved out of the house. Now I got a taste of how she felt when I went to New York for college. It was a lot quieter without her, but Cocoa seemed to sing louder to make up for that. This filled me with much happiness. After a trip home to pick up some belongings, Katie climbed into her jeep. Mama and I waved goodbye as she reversed out of the driveway. I took one look at Cocoa, who anticipated my next move, and we were off. Like so many times before, I pushed myself to beat Katie's lead foot.

My heart pounded as I raced up the main path, the cool wind on my face. Cocoa broke ahead as we rounded the bend to the straight section toward the giant pines, like monolithic guardians allowing us to pass. I watched her leap over a fallen tree and followed suit, ducking under the pine boughs that hid sight of the path. A quick hurdle to avoid the protruding tree roots, and we were on the road.

I stood in the middle and faced the top of the driveway, stretching my limbs into jumping jacks as the vehicle came into clear view. Katie revved the engine, a bright white grin plastered on her face. Cocoa's tail bud wiggled expectantly, and we moved to the side of the road. As the jeep stopped, my sister unrolled the window and poked her head out. "I knew you were going to do that!" Cocoa jumped up against the door. "Bye, Cokie," she said, adjusting her sunglasses.

"Drive safely. Love you!" I waved into the smokey dust she left behind, then started home. Cocoa sprinted ahead of me once again and waited at the intersection of the paths, a big piece of kindling perfectly balanced in her mouth. I laughed and flailed out my arms like a zombie, chasing her in the fading light of day.

Mama and I started walking together with Cocoa. I had always been close with my mother, and I treasured this quality time we shared more often now, filled with insightful conversations that inspired me. I was getting to know her better as she was becoming a dear friend. There were many similarities between us. She understood my thirst for adventure, having experienced plenty of her own.

Mama had traveled and lived in Europe for a year after graduating from college and loved it so much that she planned to go back. She couldn't wait to leave her hometown that lacked the diversity and culture she had discovered abroad. But it was on a random day that determined her fate as her heart chose my father — a man who had grown up in the same town, but she hadn't met until they attended college together. And thus, my existence began.

CHAPTER THREE:
Changing Seasons

There was still wood to stack into the shed. Mama was visiting Paw at his new assisted living home, so it was a good time to get a few loads done. I bulked up and raced outside after Cocoa. The overcast sky threatened snow, my breath visible in the wintry air. Tossing pieces of wood into the wheelbarrow, I felt the cracks open in my dry hands, the leather work gloves aggravating their rawness. The cold seeped into my extremities and I cursed it. I want to live somewhere warm! I entertained the idea of settling on a tropical island with palm trees and pineapples.

Cocoa pawed through the dwindling wood pile, found a chunk of bark, and carried it over to a spot on the driveway. I swept off the caked dirt from a large corner piece and stopped to assess my progress, the half-full row meticulously stacked in puzzle-like configurations. It was simple work for me, so naturally my mind wandered, becoming muddled with the expectations for a twenty-four year old. *What am I going to do?* The last thing I wanted was to be stuck in an office for decades, sealed off from nature, devoid of my humanness.

My eyes were drawn to the woods. So many trees were barren of their once vibrant leaves, but enduringly the pines stood tall and green as if offering hope for new life. Cocoa got up and ambled across the front yard, briefly glancing my way. I was pleased with the amount I had taken out of the remaining cord, and sitting by the woodstove with a mug of hot chocolate sounded like the best reward. I pushed the wheelbarrow onto its top and brushed off my gloves, then turned to Cocoa. "I'm gonna get you!" I cried, and she skirted out of my reach. "Okay, girl, come on in. It's *so* cold!" She was right at my heels.

I threw the gloves onto the granite table by the stove and held my hands above the heat. My fingers started to thaw, the cracks on my knuckles dried with blood. I took off my shoes and returned to my patient companion who sat near the biscuit jar. I grabbed a treat, and she confidently chose the hand that held it. "Let's see if you can get this." I crouched down, quickly hiding another one under the top of my foot as she finished chewing. "Choose," I said, my fists and feet lined up. She tapped my left hand. Nothing. She tapped my right hand. Nope. "Where is it, Cokie?" Her eyes raised to meet mine. She looked at my feet and tapped the correct option. "Good girl!" I lifted my toes to reveal her prize.

The copper kettle whistled on the woodstove as I chose my favorite brown mug from the cupboard, preparing my hot drink before sitting in front of the roaring stove. There was nothing better than this type of heat, warming to the bone. I finished the glob of melted marshmallow and lay on the plywood while Cocoa stretched out by the front door where the cold drafts came in. Amidst the crackling ambience, we drifted off to sleep.

A frigid wind blew, making it too cold for a walk. Cocoa followed me, then stopped as I moved the kitchen table and chairs aside. I went to the freezer and took out the ice cube trays. "Okay,

Cokie, back it up." I directed her into the now open space. She barked excitedly as the cubes hit the floor, pouncing on the closest one just as I tried kicking it past her. Mama joined us. "Ice cube hockey!" I said. Cocoa's eyes darted back and forth as she skillfully intercepted and ate every single piece of ice.

December 27th, 2007, was a bleak winter morning. I parked my car on a side street, a ten-minute walk from my job at the State House, and grabbed my stuff. It was chilly, and as usual, my toes, fingers, and nose were cold. I pressed the crosswalk button and waited, breathing hot air into my mittens. The light changed and I walked ahead, adjusting my purse and lunch bag over my shoulder.

Suddenly, out of the corner of my eye, I saw a plow truck driving into the lane I was crossing. Everything seemed to happen in slow motion as the vehicle was too close to dodge. I caught a glimpse of a person jumping out of a car, arms waving frantically, possibly shouting to the driver, but all sound had stopped. I felt myself pivot, and the blades hit my shoulders and shins, but I did not feel any pain. As the truck came to a stop, I slid down against the concave angle and lay there, not really in my body, everything tuned out by a deafening silence.

And then the murmurs reached my ears, turning into voices, and people were all around me. A male voice kept asking if I was okay.

"Don't move her!"

"Has someone called 9-1-1?"

"Miss, can you hear me?"

I stayed on the pavement, and even though I had an awareness of my surroundings, I could not feel anything. An angry, white-haired man approached me with a cell phone held to his ear and yelled, "What hurts?" but my voice was gone.

I was motionless, witnessing the EMTs move my body onto a board as they positioned me into a neck brace.

The ambulance ride was a blur as I stared at the ceiling of the vehicle. I could hear the wailing of the siren. There was moving and shifting as I was put onto a stretcher and rolled along a corridor in the hospital. Through all of this, I felt a tremendous sense of peace. I waited in a room and watched a handsome doctor arrive to assess my injuries. A little voice arose from me, but it didn't seem to be mine. "I was going to work... The truck hit me, I think my back and legs..."

Nurses came in and out, holding charts and peering at me. My aunt Debbie, who also worked for the state government, came into the room and held my hand. "I spoke with your mom, Amanda, she's on her way," she reassured me. All I could do was wait.

As soon as I heard Mama's voice, emotion bubbled through me and I started crying. She wiped my tears and held my face to calm me. I was taken to get a CAT scan, and as the doughnut-shaped machine went over the lower half of my body, I got the feeling that I had wet my pants. The look on my face must have given it away. "Oh, don't worry, the process makes you think that, but you're dry!" the bubbly nurse said, making me giggle. I was taken to a different room where my legs and back were X-rayed.

As the doctor examined my test results, I waited on the gurney in a hallway. A nurse came out to give me a tetanus shot, and finally, the doctor walked over and delivered the miraculous news — nothing was broken. There was some evident nerve damage and bruising, but other than that, the prognosis was positive. I was helped into a wheelchair and discharged.

Home was where I wanted to be. Mama braced me as I walked toward the house. I felt the stiffness and aching in my entire body. Cocoa was at the door, crying with happiness to see us, and I momentarily forgot about the pain. She showered me with kisses as I rested on the downstairs couch, propped up with pillows and blankets.

The singing tea kettle woke me from my nap, and I slowly sat up to welcome a cup from Mama. I fell into bouts of deep sleep for the rest of the day. As night set in, I wanted to see the stars from my bed. Cautiously, I held onto the bannister going up the stairs, Mama by my side, one step at a time. I smiled to see Cocoa already waiting at the top.

I awoke in a sweat. I could not stop the accident from replaying in my head, but instead of the truck stopping, it was plowing over my face and body as I just lay there watching it happen, helpless in preventing it. The deep-rooted fear and anxiety was all-consuming.

The next day, I received a call from the senator I worked for. "Take all the time you need to recover, Amanda," she said. "I'll be just fine in the office." She also mentioned that she had spoken with another senator who was also an attorney, and he was interested in my case. *My case.* I felt sick at the thought of going through a long-winded court battle.

The phone rang again, and it was a police officer requesting me to go to the station to file an accident report. This was all too much for me to process, and I could feel my belly shaking as the welled-up emotion surfaced. Out of felt obligation to the law and dismissing how sore I was, I agreed to go in and get it over with. I hugged Cocoa, and as if sensing my weakness, she gave a single lick to my face and watched me leave.

"How're you feeling?" Mama asked as she drove.

"Sore and upset. I just can't stop envisioning what would have happened if he didn't hit the brakes… But it's weird because I can't remember the feeling of the impact. I can't remember *feeling* anything. It was like I was out of my body watching myself." Mama was quiet before responding.

"I think you definitely had an angel with you," she said, "like when Paw had his accident." I would never forget that day. I was at unicycling practice and heard my father had double-vision and crashed into a utility pole. He hadn't known the electricity line came down right outside his truck door. "Miraculously, he stepped over the live wire when he got out of the crew-cab," Mama recalled. "He turned to see what had slid from under the seat and hit his feet during the crash, and it was a framed picture that read 'Guardian Angel.' " Yes, that resonated with me. Just as Paw had been, I, too, was divinely protected.

In the stark police department, I slowly completed the report, trying to detail it as much as I could. In my recollections, I was reliving the experience and all the emotions attached to it. I felt nauseous and handed the form to the uninterested receptionist. Eager to distance myself from there, we headed home.

It was consoling for me to be in the peace and quiet of the woods with Mama and Cocoa. Days went by and I lay in bed, Cocoa watching me intently as if trying to encourage me, *will me* to get up and move. The bruises on my shins were big and painful, and my back seemed to creak with aching ripples. I was going to begin physical therapy and hoped it would help.

When I returned to work a week later, I could see the attorney senator sizing me up, and I couldn't help but feel that he was looking for dollar signs in my injuries. "Amanda, I'd like to meet with you and discuss what happened," he said as I hobbled out of the Senate Chamber on crutches. The proceedings started, and the details of the accident were disclosed from both sides. What I was about to hear would pose an inner battle for me.

"He is denying responsibility and claims you were crossing on the wrong light," the lawyer stated. My heart sank.

"How could he? *I* had the signal to cross. *He* was supposed to yield to me as a pedestrian, the sign near the light even indicates that!" I felt my anger boil and build like I was going to explode. I went home feeling the injustice of it and couldn't comprehend being blamed for getting hurt when I *knew* I had followed the law.

My physical therapy sessions went well, but as those bodily pains dissipated, the anger continued to well up. I faced dense emotions. I spent countless nights trying to understand how someone so obviously in the wrong could blatantly lie about it. Soon after, some photos were submitted by the police that revealed tall snow piles blocking the pedestrian crossing button to signal the light change. They hadn't been there on that fateful morning, but the lawyer still dropped my case.

I knew there was something crooked about the whole situation, but I was helpless in proving anything. My honesty wasn't enough. The only escape I had, the only time my anger would subside was when I'd walk with Cocoa through the snow of winter. The blank canvas seemed to hit an internal reset button, the cold reminding me I was alive. I watched her run ahead, acting as she always did, turning to make sure I was there. Her playful energy was refreshing. The love I experienced in those moments was exactly the support I needed, the verification that I had so much to be thankful for.

⇾

Aside from some recurring numbness in my upper back, I physically recovered from the accident. My emotional recovery was an ongoing issue. I finally tried writing a letter to the driver of the plow truck, as the simple act of writing how I felt started to release some of that anger. I came to the realization that the only way I could move on from the trauma was to forgive. I never sent the letter. The fear that this man must have faced was not an excuse for his actions, but through it, I was taught a tremendous life lesson in order to heal. *Forgiveness* was the answer.

⇾

As I sat on the dock looking out at the melting pond with Cocoa in tow, the sun emerged from the cloudy sky and I immediately was grateful. Grateful that through all of this, I was shown the light — the light shone on me in choosing forgiveness. I could literally *walk* away. The epiphany continued. Everything happened for a greater purpose and I needed to learn more, to grow more. Australia lingered in my thoughts. Could I revisit that foreign land that had captivated me so much? Could I quit my job and sell my car? Then, the tug at my heart strings. Would I be able to leave Cocoa for an adventure on my own?

⇾

I was running my first 5K race. As I pushed my body, a noticeable weight lifted. I moved with ease and endurance, my lungs welcoming the influx of oxygen, my cells stimulated with vitality. I was leaving my job, had sold my car and just been granted a working holiday visa to Australia. I was moving forward all by myself.

I caught Cocoa's eye while I was deep in thought. My biggest luggage, backpack, and various piles of things were strewn around my room as I attempted packing. I had enough practice from living in France for a trimester in high school, my five years at college, and then my first trip to Australia after graduation. This should be easy. I had organized most of my stuff, but it felt like I was missing something.

Cocoa walked over to me and swung her bum to hit my side, asking for a rub. I scratched her and she wiggled back and forth. "You're my good girl," I said. I could feel the love exuding from her. Then it suddenly dawned on me. I had been with her since she was a puppy, and this would be my first time being separated from her. *She* was the missing element I couldn't take with me.

I close my eyes and feel the wind sweep my face. I love the wind. It takes me through the seasonal changes that dictate where we are in the year. In the winter, it snaps into a chilling guise, one that refreshes and enlivens. As it frosts the earth, glazing the newly fallen snow into a glittery gloss, I am invigorated and present in its boldness.

When the chill has ached my bones and I've had enough, a gentler breeze brings the glorious sound of icicles dripping, increasing the tempo as new life awakens. The perfumed blossoms of spring whirl in, and I look up to see a formation of geese glide above.

Then, the balmy currents carry the sweet notes of wild strawberries and dried grass of summer while the sounds of grasshoppers and moths and distant bird calls throughout the forest are delivered to my ears in a most entrancing collaboration. I watch the breeze ripple across the pond, creating undulating patterns until it seems to take a breath of momentary stillness before changing direction.

The air begins to turn, still warm but with the subtle undertones of a deepening transition into coolness. The acorns are given the nudge to drop, and I can almost taste the earthy maple of the falling leaves of autumn.

The wind has now brought me to a new season where I will find more meaning and significance in a faraway world.

CHAPTER FOUR:
A New Adventure

As the plane began to taxi toward the runway, I couldn't help but feel a little unsure. I was leaving my comfort zone in the woods, the place where I found such contentment and peace, and my best friend with whom I shared it with. Was I abandoning her? My human family understood what was happening, but I knew it wasn't the same for Cocoa. Leaving her really struck a chord in my heart.

I replayed the final moments at home, hugging that precious ball of boisterous love, knowing it would probably be the last time I could pick her up like a teddy bear. As I gazed into her curious yellow eyes, she lapped my face and watched me wheel out my luggage. The tears were rolling down my cheeks, and I needed to say one more goodbye. I ran inside to wrap my arms around her, kissing her face and holding her close. She took a biscuit from my hand and chewed it quickly, gave me a long look, and went into the living room. I tore myself from her, trying to keep in mind that I was only going to be away for a year.

The trip already seemed longer than I remembered, perhaps because I was doubting my decision. My heart and my head were in conflict. What was I really doing? Was I simply trying to put off the "real world" of being an adult, holding down a regular job, and doing all the predictable things that appeared to be the way of life? Maybe I feared responsibility. Regardless of the reason, I couldn't ignore the undeniable pull I felt in another direction. There was something I needed, but I had no idea what. I just knew I had to return to Australia. Round Two. My soul was searching for more. There had to be *more*.

Mama had given me a letter, and I studied her writing on the envelope, "Read on plane." It was her tradition to write to me for every big trip — a true gift I would look forward to, wondering what heartfelt words of wisdom she would bestow upon me. *Wait until the big plane, until I am way above the Pacific Ocean*, I thought to myself. I watched the puzzle of land below as the plane chased the sunset across the country.

In the international terminal, I made a quick call home. My mother's cheerful voice answered. "Hi, Mama! I'm in L.A.," I said. "One flight down, one to go!"

"Great! Make sure you eat some healthy food before you board, you know what those plane meals are like." She paused. "Cocoa is pretty confused. She keeps looking around your room and then wants to go outside. She realizes something's up." I felt a pang of sadness and guilt.

"Can you give her a big hug for me? I left the *Frog and Toad* book on my night table if you want to read it to her."

"Yes, and I will try to take her to all the places you do," Mama reassured me. "We'll be fine, don't worry."

"Okay… Thanks so much. Well, I'd better let you go to bed. I'll call when I'm there." We said our goodbyes.

On the big plane, I found my preferred window seat in the back. Already dressed in comfy clothes, I organized my stuff and got settled. No one was seated next to me yet. I watched other passengers find their seats, and upon hearing some Australian accents, my anticipated adventure started to sink in. A voice came over the speakers to initiate the takeoff protocol.

It was just me in the row. I tried to contain my excitement but couldn't help smiling. I would get to stretch out and sleep on the seats, and for fifteen hours, sleep was a good way to pass some time. Before long we were in the air, and I opened my bag to take out Mama's letter. Several hundred dollar bills were carefully folded inside. No matter how little she earned, she always seemed to have some set aside for her loved ones.

My Dearest Amandy, what an adventure you are going to have! I am so happy that you have decided to travel once more to the land that inspired you. Know that all will be well here at home. I will give Cocoa plenty of attention, and she will be okay. You will see each other again. There are so many exciting things that are in store for you. I am proud of your independent nature, and your journey will be everything you make it. Be safe. God bless. We love you.

- Mama, Paw, and Cokie

I reread her words and kissed the letter, snuggled onto the seats, and dozed off to sleep.

After almost thirty hours of travel between car, bus, domestic and international planes, I arrived at Sydney Airport and made my way through the customs checkpoint, completely exhausted and ready to sleep on a real bed. I took out the money Mama had tucked into her letter and exchanged it for the colorful Monopoly-like notes, then proceeded to the trains. My backpack weighed heavily on my tired body, and I was already eager to set it down.

The train sped through a dark tunnel, and I caught my reflection in the window. For as self-sufficient as I was, it was strange to see myself alone. In the short time Cocoa had been part of my life, I had gotten used to her being by my side, accompanying me on all of my adventures. I felt her absence as if I was missing a limb and definitely held onto some regret about leaving her.

I quickly gathered my belongings and got off at the next stop. The heat and humidity hit me as soon as I stepped onto the sidewalk, worsening on my trek to the closest youth hostel. "We are full, but the YHA might have space," the guy at the front desk told me.

Then I remembered the vacancy sign I had just seen going by an Irish pub. Every step on my return was grueling as I trudged along with my big backpack on my back and little one on my front while pulling my luggage behind me. I was like a mule in the blazing midday sun. *Why couldn't I have packed lighter?* I didn't really need so much stuff. Surely I would find somewhere to store my extra possessions to lessen my load.

I finally reached the pub and went inside. It was dimly lit, and an eighties rock song was playing. The bartender looked at my burden and quickly nodded. "You want a room, hey?" I shook my head and offered him a fifty dollar note. "This way, I've got a single with a bathroom." I followed him upstairs where he unlocked a door. "Check-out is at eleven," he said as he left.

The room was clean, and I quickly let the backpacks slide from my shoulders to rest against the wall by my luggage. I turned on the radio and unpacked my toiletries, then put on my flip flops and took perhaps the best shower in my life before settling on the bed. My thoughts drifted to Cocoa, and a tear rolled down my cheek as I drifted off to sleep.

I awoke the next morning, refreshed and with a clear mind. I needed cheaper accommodation while I figured out what to do with my bags and where I was headed. I ducked out to Woolworths and got some fruit and yogurt for breakfast, then found a payphone nearby.

"Hi, Mama! I got in yesterday and spent the night in my own room, in an Irish pub of all places!" She chuckled.

"Have you exchanged the money I gave you?"

"Yes, thank you so much. That was incredibly generous of you." I paused. "How's Cocoa?"

"She's still searching the house, sniffing where your bags were, and jumps onto your bed and stares out the window. She undoubtedly misses you." Mama sighed. "I'm doing my best to cheer her up, but it'll definitely take some adjustment." The red double-decker tour bus going by distracted me from the lingering sadness and guilt I felt in leaving my dear friend.

"Please give her kisses for me. I'll be in touch once I get my feet on the ground." After hanging up, I realized that the only way I could begin my adventure was not to look back.

⇁

I met Maria at the hostel down the street. She was an outgoing Italian who was taking a break from work to explore Sydney. "It's too crowded in there," she said as I waited for her to clear the door. "I'm searching for another place if you want to join me," she offered, seeing I was alone. I peered in to observe the party atmosphere in the cramped lounge area and nodded back.

I recalled my first experience in Byron Bay when I spent a night in a room with eight bunks at full capacity, awoken by conversations, loud snoring, and others coming in and out at all hours. That type of environment wasn't for me. Maybe I was more grown up than I thought. On a street near the Irish pub, we came across a decent, clean, and quiet accommodation, albeit a little pricier. I also found a locker to store my large backpack and left some things behind.

For the next few days, Maria and I toured around Sydney by train, ferry, on foot, and on the red bus. At Circular Quay, street performers of all kinds lined the wharves to dazzle, puzzle, and entertain. An Aboriginal man with bright dot art painted all over his body played a didgeridoo, so profoundly communicating the pulse of Australia, I could feel its vibration in my bones.

On the packed ferry to Manly Beach, we had astonishing views. The Sydney Harbour Bridge exhibited tiny figures of people climbing it, while the Sydney Opera House stood prominently, an architectural masterpiece with its dynamic angles. It was a pleasant ride on the water, and we arrived at the popular destination happy and relaxed.

The boardwalk was crowded with an eclectic mix of suntanned beach bums, backpackers, families, pet-owners, locals, and artists. It felt like a safe and free community where everyone basked in the elements. After spending the day in the concentrated warmth of the sun, the rhythmic surf lulling us to sleep, we boarded the ferry again. The sky was soft pink, and I was filled with wonder of what would come.

I decided to take a train to Brisbane to see what was there. An elderly couple sat a few rows ahead of me. When I got up to use the lavatory, I smiled at them as the woman took out a precisely packed sandwich to share with her husband. She returned my smile. "Are you traveling alone?" she asked.

"Yes. I'm on a working holiday visa, so I can earn money to supplement my adventures."

"Isn't that terrific," she said. "Herb and I have gone all around Australia. There's so much to see! Been married fifty-five years now." I was in awe of their commitment, the twinkle in their eyes when they looked at each other. I briefly pondered what it would be like to have someone to share my life with.

I wished them well as they got off at Casino, New South Wales. I had worked at an organic coffee farm not far from there. The rolling countryside was so lush and picturesque, maybe I should reconsider my plans... But surely the city would have more opportunities for paid work. I had to get to a computer to see what was available.

The "River City" was busy and people didn't seem very friendly. I located a nearby hostel and dropped my stuff in a four-share room before finding a computer. Other people were on the same search. "Try Gumtree," a girl said with a German accent, "it's a marketplace for everything."

"Thank you." I clicked through many postings and discovered most paying jobs were up north. I logged onto my email and reached out to a few contacts, then went to check the public bulletin board. It didn't have much aside from carpool ads. I found the payphone and called home.

"What's it like so far?" Mama had an excited tone in her voice, and I knew she was living vicariously through me. After all, she loved a good adventure.

"I met a girl named Maria. We ended up staying together and toured around the iconic sites in Sydney. All the trees are blossoming and the air is so fragrant!" I paused.

"Sounds marvelous! Just the opposite here. It's getting chillier and our first snowstorm has been forecasted." I smiled as I thought about the snow.

"Cocoa is going to love that. Can I say a quick hello to her?"

"Sure. Let me stretch this cord to reach her under the table." I heard a brief scuffling sound. "Okay, it's up to her ear." I closed my eyes and imagined her sweet face.

"Cokie! Hi, girl, it's Mandy, it's *just me*! I miss you so much…" I said.

"Oh, she's getting up and going to the door. She thinks you're here. Wait a minute while I let her out." My heart sank and I just wanted to reassure her that I would return. I waited. "So, what now?" Mama asked.

"I'm in Brisbane, but not sure it's for me. It's dismal, maybe because I'm only seeing skyscrapers… And I haven't felt much warmth from people. I've started looking for work, but it's all farming jobs in exchange for accommodation like I did last time. I need to make money so I can explore more, otherwise I won't be able to afford it." She was quiet for a moment.

"Do you want to come home?"

I pictured the snowy winter that was right around the corner and snowshoeing in the woods with Cocoa in the silence of the cold. *Cold*. Then I thought of my raw knuckles cracking open and bleeding and remembered my wish to live in a warm climate. The plow accident was surely a catalyst for making a change. I had nothing to lose by staying longer. A year would pass quickly, and I definitely felt more grounded now.

"No, I owe it to myself to stick it out. I just don't want to be in a city. I am going to go north, see if I can find something in Airlie Beach again." The gateway to the Whitsunday Islands must have some kind of work for me.

"Okay. Keep me posted," Mama said. "Good luck. Remember it's the *adventure* you wanted, so enjoy the ride!"

I was glad she reminded me of that. I was only a week into my trip and had enough money to sustain me for a while, so why stress about work right away? I checked out of the hostel, walked the few blocks to Roma Street Station, and boarded the next train north. This was going to be an overnight journey. The cityscape turned into rural bushland, and kangaroos hopped along in the distant fields under the setting sun. I smiled as my eyelids grew heavy.

―⁊―

Airlie Beach didn't appeal to me anymore, maybe because I had changed. The beach scene by day and party by night was fun when I was a recent graduate, but years later, I appreciated getting sleep and taking better care of myself. Now, even amongst the busy tourists, it just seemed lonely to me. The bed and breakfast I had worked at was renovated by new owners, but aside from that, the whole town appeared to be trapped in time.

I sat on the beach, staring out at the bay, deliberating my next move. The "ACHTUNG!" warning sign for crocodiles was posted in the same area. It was such a disappointment to have that danger when the water looked so inviting. Looks most certainly can be deceiving. That said, I decided to give Airlie Beach another chance and checked into a hostel for the night.

My new mobile phone woke me. It was Patrick, an Aussie acquaintance from home, and he had a connection. "His name is David and he needs a P.A.," he said. "I told him you worked for a senator, and he was very interested." He gave me his number. I thanked him and called his contact, feeling my stomach quiver with nervous excitement as the phone rang.

"Hello," a friendly voice answered, and I introduced myself. David had an event space and kitchen he hired out, a hole-in-the-wall coffee shop, a catering company, as well as a few other projects going on, so he needed someone to assist him. It sounded like a good opportunity.

"I'd be happy to! I'm up at Airlie Beach but can get on a train right away."

"That's great, I look forward to meeting you in person then. Let's give it the weekend and start fresh on Monday, does that sound alright?" he asked. I was in. After we hung up, I checked the schedule for a bus to the train station. I had a job, and of all places, back in Brisbane.

I found a hostel not far from where I would work in West End, an artsy cultural community with a strong Greek presence. I organized my things, picking out the best clothing I had for my first day. It took me twenty minutes to walk to the business location, and I paused to dab the sweat on my face before approaching. A man waved at me from a table in front of the building.

David was a creative businessman with an interesting history, and very quickly, I knew we would get along well. I worked in a laidback environment with varying responsibilities, from managing the coffee shop to organizing the office. The catering team shared the space for administration duties, and I became close to Helen, a kind and nurturing woman in her forties.

One morning before work, I heard my phone beeping. I hadn't used it since Airlie Beach. There was a voicemail from Katie, and she sounded off. "I'm so sorry to leave a message like this on your phone, but it's the only way to reach you. Grampa died. They found him in bed. Call me or Mama if you can. Love you."

I was completely shocked. Grampa had just been at my bon voyage party and seemed fine, aside from some swelling in his legs. I remembered my frustration when he asked me to wrap his ankles with an Ace bandage, and I ignored his request. Angry tears began to flow as I regretted my selfishness and wished I had helped him. That was the last time I saw him.

I called Mama, who was clearly grief-stricken. No one knew how her father died, only that he had gone a couple of days prior to being found. An upcoming surgery had inevitably been weighing on him. He lived alone for eight years after my grandmother died, and silently, it was thought that he feared the procedure would take away that independence. That he had gone peacefully on his own terms.

However consoling the notion, it was overpowered by the suddenness of his death, and I sat alone crying. What was I to do now? Should I go home for his funeral and to be with my family? I was distraught and called David to tell him the news. "I understand, you do what you need to," he said sympathetically.

I decided to stay in Brisbane. If I went home, this solo adventure would most likely be over and I hadn't found the "more" part yet. I went to a Catholic chapel in the city. No one was around. It felt safe and comforting to be there, and I walked up to the lectern and faced the empty pews. I spoke from my heart about my grandfather.

"And I'll never forget how he melted when he held Cocoa as a puppy, you see, for as guarded as he appeared to be, he was full of love—" A man walked into the back of the chapel and took one look at me before departing as quickly as he had arrived. I finished my eulogy, then lit a candle for Grampa and bowed my head in prayer.

⁓

Everyone was so supportive when I returned to work. Helen took me aside. "Are you still staying in the hostel, honey?" I nodded. "Well, I have a rumpus room I can rent out to you. There's a toilet and shower down the hall, and you can share our kitchen upstairs. It's a quiet neighborhood, close to a creek walk, bike circuit, shops, airport, and public transport." It sounded like luxury compared to where I was living and didn't take me long to consider her offer. The next morning, I moved out of the hostel.

Nundah was a nice town, or "suburb" as I learned to call it. Helen's house was on a cul-de-sac, and a flourishing poinciana tree stood at the front. I had a large living area on the ground level, with glass doors looking out at a backyard screened in by various shrubbery. There was a mattress on the floor, an old wooden armoire for my clothes, and a couch. Plenty of room for my scant possessions. Helen and her two daughters lived upstairs with their fox terrier, and I was readily welcomed into their family.

Helen drove me to work until I figured out the best way to get there on my own. It seemed long at first. A walk, a train, two buses, and the final walk to the office generally took more than an hour, but I got used to it. It was good exercise and thinking time. On a grassy shortcut near my new place, I regularly passed a gated and fenced-in yard around a quaint brick house, with the other poinciana on the street proudly stretching its branches above the lawn.

One day, a beautiful black and white border collie came running to the gate barking, immediately catching my attention. I walked over to say hello. She relaxed as I petted her, and I could see the tag on her collar. "Nice to meet you, Holly," I said. "My name is Amanda." She was dainty-looking. A little black spot resembling a beauty mark was on her muzzle, and her black nose gleamed when her tongue swept across it. Her ears came to a crimped curve at their tips. She was mostly black with a fully white collar and chest, while shimmery auburn parts throughout her coat were highlighted by the sun. She had an athletic but smaller build than Cocoa, and boy was she fast!

She did circuits around the yard and under the front hedge when a delivery truck revved down the street. I thought it was sad she wasn't on a property where she could run freely. My mind wandered to Cocoa and how fortunate she was in the woods. She wouldn't like being confined. But if Holly grew up only knowing this limited space, maybe it was better than getting a taste of ultimate freedom.

On Christmas Day, 2008, I met Holly's owner. He was the handsome blond guy walking along the street as Helen, the girls, and I rode back from their family's holiday party. "You have to meet him!" Helen rolled down the windows. "Hey, Matty, how ya goin'?" This dashing stranger peered in and we were introduced. I noticed him checking me out, and I was glad to be wearing a pretty dress. His sea green eyes had an unmissable twinkle in them.

"Just headed to my parents," he said, lingering for a minute before wishing us a Merry Christmas. A few days later, I was walking past his house and stopped to pat Holly. When I looked up, he was standing by the door and gave me a big wave. I shyly returned the gesture and continued on.

It was the beginning of the new year when I saw Matt again. Unbeknownst to me, he had spoken with Helen and arranged a visit. He sat at the dining table eating some leftover potato salad while I was on the computer, messaging a guy I had dated just before my trip. "So, how do you like living here?" he piped up.

"It's alright. I'm not used to being in suburbia though, the houses are all so packed together," I said. "But Helen has really made me feel at home. I have my own space too, so I can't complain other than my back being sore from the mattress."

"I have a spare one if you want it. It's fairly comfortable," he offered.

"That would be great, thank you!" Our eyes locked until the sound of a new message broke the moment.

"Do you want to go to dinner tonight?" he asked abruptly. I was taken aback and stopped typing, my heart racing. I wasn't used to being put on the spot and couldn't come up with an excuse not to.

"Okay."

"How about seven o'clock?" He scraped the last bite of food from the plate.

"Sounds good."

"If you want, you can have the mattress now." I nodded and got up to accompany him to his house. As the gate opened, Holly greeted me excitedly before running off and returning with a ball. She dropped it in front of me and ran to the grass, crouching low with eagle-eye focus. I threw it, and in one swift movement, she retrieved it, dropping it at my feet once again.

"She'll do that all day," Matt said. I had never met a border collie until Holly. I petted her, then entered the tidy house. There wasn't a picture on the wall, and the leather sectional, a desk, and a chair was the only furniture in the dining and living areas. We sat down, seemingly forgetting the reason why I had come over.

We became totally engrossed in conversation. I wanted to know more about Australian wildlife — the snakes, crocodiles, kangaroos, and koalas, while Matt was fascinated with the larger animals from my home. He listened intently as I told him of my hikes, running through the woods, and swimming in freshwater. "Aren't you afraid of being attacked by a bear?" he asked, clearly concerned.

"No, not really," I said. "I always have my dog, Cocoa, with me. She's an Australian shepherd. Go figure, she's an Aussie and I'm the one in Australia!" I laughed. "Anyway, most animals will catch her scent and run off. She's my eyes and ears... And my best friend." My heart ached from missing her. How far away she was.

The late afternoon sun was setting, and I glanced at my watch. I had to get ready for our date soon. On the walk back to Helen's, I couldn't help but think of what a pleasant surprise this guy was. He was really interesting to converse with, so intrigued by the world I came from. Judging from our first visit, it was easy to lose track of time with him.

We went to an Italian restaurant for dinner, and for some reason, I wasn't nervous. It was like I already knew my date. The conversation continued, and we started talking about Matt's love for fishing. He had his own boat and described all the places he went. "Maybe sometime you can go with me?" he posed. I nodded. *Maybe.*

I perused the menu, full of seafood options I had never heard of, until my eyes noticed something familiar — salmon. "Snapper is tasty," Matt suggested. He was the expert.

"Okay. The snapper, please," I told the waiter.

"Salmon, thanks," Matt said, then turned to me. "If you don't like the snapper, you can have the salmon." I wasn't used to this thoughtfulness from a guy. Matt excused himself, and my phone rang. Who could be calling me? I quickly picked up and heard my eldest brother's voice.

"Hey, James! I'm on a date right now, sorry I can't talk," I whispered.

"No problem, Mandy. That's cool."

"Yeah, he seems really great! We'll catch up in a bit," I said. Matt returned to the table right after I hung up and smiled at me.

It only took that first date and I just knew. It was as if our story had been written in a romance novel — "Girl travels to foreign land and falls for the boy next door…" I spent less and less time at Helen's, having dinner with Matt almost every night. Soon he left me a key, and I walked Holly on a regular basis.

She was so eager to exercise, and I loved taking her out to the parklands all around us. Ibises fished along the sandbanks of the tidal creek, their long beaks instruments of precision. We ducked through a hidden shortcut to sports fields and dodged the plovers who claimed much of the open space while they protected their young. I couldn't take my eyes off the fig trees, like goliaths with their massive trunks and sprawling crowns.

Holly was in her element, running and stalking the ball until we sat to catch our breath. Swallows dive-bombed the various insects that came out as the heat from the day dissipated. I couldn't help but giggle when willie wagtails landed near me, wiggling their tail feathers back and forth, reminding me of Cocoa's beloved greeting.

Our next rest stop was in my favorite section of the park on the way home. We watched the magpies seek nourishment in the grass as the bush turkeys went about their business, scraping up earthen matter for their mounded nests. I got used to scanning the landscape for snakes. The kookaburras laughed as dusk approached, and I stopped to spot them high up in the branches. Despite being in suburbia, I was indeed living in Australia.

Not long after I began dating Matt, I met his neighbors, Peter and Kathy. They were warm and caring, and we became close. Peter had a special bond with Holly, and without fail, he whistled to her at the end of every day to give her biscuits. I observed from the kitchen window as she ran to him, offering her paws while he tried to smuggle in a pat before she raced off to find a ball.

There was a rivalry between Holly and the magpies they loved. With her head held low, she focused on the birds who had come for their daily feeding of raw meat. She watched and whimpered with disapproval, staring them down as Peter reached his hand out. Sometimes they taunted her by walking close to the fence or landing on it, and in those instances, she would stalk them and wait until her intense stance seemed to scare them away.

The extreme heat of summer started turning. I couldn't wait for the end of each work day when I commuted home to see Matt and Holly. I spent most of my weekends with them. Through my influence, Holly was upgraded to sleeping in the house instead of the garage. Our quality time together was unfolding. Matt exposed me to the benefits of city living with all kinds of places in reasonable proximity to us. He took me to fancy restaurants where we indulged in local, fresh, diverse cuisine.

I finally got the promised boating trip. I swallowed my nervousness and trusted Matt to keep us safely out of the potentially shark-ridden territories. We coasted along picturesque water that changed colors. Crystal clarity in the shallower depths showed starfish on the ocean floor, while a gradient of light green to dark blue was where dolphins swam at tremendous speeds, celebrating their extensive playground. Coastal birds indicated where the next school of mackerel would surface, revealing their iridescent skin that glimmered like mermaids during their brief appearance. It was so breathtakingly beautiful that my eyes couldn't take it all in. I was having an adventure of a lifetime.

At Matt's thirtieth birthday party, I officially met his family. His parents, Greg and Jenny, and younger sisters, Kate and Sarah. It was apparent that they were close, reminiscent of mine. I also met Matt's best friend, Chris, and his partner, Melina. Amongst the crowd, I watched as my jovial boyfriend blew out the candles on his cake, and the Aussie version of the birthday song concluded with "Hip hip hurray!" three times over.

I used the money from my tax return to buy a plane ticket for Katie to visit me. It was April, and the air was much cooler. I waited at Sydney Airport for my sister's arrival and couldn't miss her when she walked into the lobby. "Welcome to Australia!" I threw my arms around her.

"Thanks! Oh, it's so humid here," she said, already breaking into a sweat.

"Wait 'til we get to tropical Queensland," I warned. Katie had ten days with me, and I had planned them to the max. We checked into the youth hostel I had previously stayed at, then went out to eat. "Feel like a little sightseeing today?" I was unsure of how much energy she had after the big trip.

"Okay, but I think I need a little nap first," she said. We walked back to the room where she dozed off into the afternoon. At last she stirred, and I looked up from my book to see her awaken.

"There's so much to see, but if you'd prefer to keep it simple tonight, we can get a fresh start tomorrow," I said. She agreed. We stayed in and had a much-needed talk. She told me about living with her boyfriend, Mike, and I raved about Matt. It was new that both of us were in relationships.

Revived by morning, we hopped on the city tour bus and took in the attractions. "I never imagined I'd visit this city so much, and now we're here together!" I said. "Do you remember watching the Sydney Olympics at Grampa's and thinking Australia was so far away?"

"Yes!" Katie paused in quiet contemplation. "I still can't believe Grampa's gone. It was only last Thanksgiving he was sitting in our living room. I was upset about something and went upstairs. He left shortly after. I had a voicemail from him, apologizing for not saying goodbye and he hoped I was okay." She sighed. "That was the last time I saw and heard from him. He died so unexpectedly, I don't feel like we had any closure. In a way, it's as if he's still around." We shared a tearful moment.

"I know. I had this really cute postcard I was going to send him before Christmas but waited to mail it. He would have gotten a kick out of it too. I just wish we could see him again."

Katie giggled in recollection. "Remember when he sat on the bench in our yard with chubby little Cocoa on his lap? He had the gentlest smile as he picked her up, trying to get her to pose for the camera. He was like a little boy with her." We sat there in the ambience of Manly Wharf that afternoon, eating rich Swiss ice cream while recalling fond memories of our grandfather.

I was trying to navigate our rental car that had a GPS voice with an Australian accent. "Lara," we called her. She was difficult to understand, and the metric system wasn't helping matters. I think I broke half a dozen road rules as we crawled through the city, eventually finding the highway south toward Wollongong. Luckily, it was smooth sailing from there.

We stopped in a charming coastal town. "Those trees are like huge pineapples!" Katie said, pointing to mammoth replicas of her favorite fruit.

"Just for you." I snapped a photo. Dozens of pelicans were by the dockside of a seafood restaurant, cartoonlike as they turned to look at us. The light blue sky was streaked with wispy clouds, then became overcast when we reached the blindingly white beach of Jervis Bay. As she squinted at my camera, I felt so grateful to be sharing this wonderland with my little sister.

Helen threw a party to welcome Katie to Brisbane. Everyone liked her, which did not surprise me. She had a way of making people feel happy with a smile that could brighten a dismal day. It was so much fun to be together, and she and Matt joked sarcastically as though they were old friends. With all the newness of everything, Katie could see how different my life had become.

Up north, we went on the Skyrail to visit the mountain village of Kuranda and later took a guided tour to the Daintree. The rainforest's lush greenery and virgin waterways drew us in as we sat on rocks, gazing at a scene that seemed airbrushed into wild perfection. Upon approaching the beaches, the "ACHTUNG!" warning signs for crocodiles were posted everywhere. These strips were superficially deceitful with their alluring beauty, ruled by prehistoric-looking creatures lurking in the shallows. While having lunch at a nearby picnic area, we were shocked when a human-sized goanna ran up the tree beside us!

It was already hot the next morning when we took a tour boat out to a section of the Great Barrier Reef. "Anyone want a noodle?" one of the crew members offered. I wasn't confident in the ocean, so I grabbed a couple. We jumped in after the group, soon peering through goggles at the splendor below. Everything was represented in different textures, depths, and life forms, and we were immersed in our own underwater discoveries.

A big, pillow-like form, nude in color, billowed amongst the coral. We broke to the surface, laughing hysterically until we saw the current had drifted us. A reef shark swam far below, his eyes to the side in a suspicious-looking stare, while right in front of us was nothing but darkness. The deep ocean. We quickly resurfaced and searched for the rest of the snorkelers, frantically making distance from the unknown.

The severity of the Australian sun revealed itself that night when Katie suffered its painful wrath, sunburned and heat-exhausted. I rushed out to find some aloe vera to soothe her inflamed skin. I realized that in my wanting to give her a wonderful experience of the country, I had thrown caution to the wind and pushed her too far. Perhaps it was my relentless desire to have more adventure.

Fraser Island was undoubtedly proving to share its popularity with Katie. She seemed revitalized as we rode along the beach in a jacked-up bus. The driver swerved around the amoeba-like spans of exposed coffee rock that marbled the sand with its gray-black contrast. The rough surf was dangerous, teeming with sharks just behind its breakpoint. Charging forward, we beat the rising tide to make it to Indian Head for widespread ocean views.

"Turtles!" someone said, the circular bodies unmistakable from our lookout. *Click click* went the cameras. Descending to the beach, we waded into the lucent water softly swirling in all directions. The sun beat down as the tour continued to the Maheno shipwreck. Its rusty frame was akin to the red sand of Australia, strange in its vast presence on the otherwise uninterrupted shoreline.

The bus brought us to Eli Creek, the final stop for the day. The bases of the trees along the boardwalk looked like piles of paintbrushes, as if an artist had put his tools aside after creating the scene we jumped into. We floated amidst the teal-tinged freshwater as leisurely as the afternoon and the snake who swam near the banking. Then it was back to our accommodation for the night, secured to keep out the dingoes who posed a danger to naïve tourists desperate for a photo.

The remainder of the trip was spent inland. The famous perched lakes bewitched us with their vibrancy of color, fine silica sand, and soothing water. We walked around enormous vines entangled and draped into the rainforest paths. A warm rain showered us, so sweet and unforgettable of a memory in the natural paradise. We had truly explored the diverse landscapes of the largest sand island in the world.

⇁

Katie left with a distinct feeling of Australia — the rural beauty and the contrasting liveliness of the city-suburban side. Meeting Matt was a bonus. As we watched her board the plane, I was happy she had made this trek. She would now return to her love, clear on where her life was headed. I, on the other hand, had no idea about my future.

⇁

I crouched down to hold the side of the boat while Matt parked his ute and trailer. *Ding ding.* The masts on the pontoons indicated the sea breeze, which off the water was warm and harmless. My skin was already absorbing the intensifying morning rays. Pelicans waited for the fish scraps at the filleting station, but they weren't the only ones. Crows claimed their share with clicks and guttural sounds as seagulls patrolled from the air currents above.

The water sloshed against the boat, and swimming close to the surface in masses were blue jellyfish, their tentacles flailing about with the increasing tide. Cocoa would surely be intrigued by them just as I was. I felt myself slip into a trance, watching their rhythmic movement until Matt returned. His face was serious with concentration as the engine turned over easily and gurgled the water. I untied the front of the boat and climbed in.

Music played as we sped across the flat water toward Stradbroke Island. Cormorants balanced on the beacons and I waved to them. "Dolphins," Matt pointed, but the illusions from the reflecting light tricked me and I had missed them. I looked at the ship powering through the channel, pushing droves of water, and I was glad we avoided its waves. The sheer enormity of this vessel in the bay would be dwarfed out at sea.

Matt slowed the boat to idle, then switched off the engine. We had stopped in a green zone to watch a shy dugong, the bay's sea cow, partially surface before plunging down and out of our sight. The gentle giant seemed almost as elusive as the Loch Ness Monster of Scotland. The water was bountiful with activity, a shiny school of hundreds of small fish swam toward the surface, and we heard someone swimming amongst it. The deep breaths sounded hoarse and aged as they got closer. Much to my surprise, it wasn't an elderly man, but a sea turtle cruising by.

At a restaurant on Hamilton Island, Matt reached for my hand. "When we get back to Brisbane, I want you to move in with me," he said. Butterflies filled my stomach.

"Really?" I had never taken this step. He nodded. I knew our relationship was getting serious and it felt right. "Okay!" I shouted to him over the noise of the dining room. We still had a few months left of this whirlwind of a year together. What else could possibly be in store for us?

⁓

We sailed to Whitehaven Beach. I had been there before, to those stunningly white sands with pristine water that looked turquoise in contrast. A picture could not do it justice. Matt and I walked along the immaculate beach hand in hand while the crew laid out a full spread of fresh seafood and produce, then waved us over to indulge.

The boat took us toward a stretch of reef, and our small group put on wetsuits and snorkeling gear as the early afternoon sun illuminated the water. Matt was a natural swimmer and jumped right in, disappearing under the surface. I took my time, trying not to think about sharks and my apprehension in the ocean, especially without a noodle or anyone close by. I adjusted my goggles and finally slid off the side.

As I swam above the colorful coral and the fish inhabiting it, the water got shallower and shallower and I couldn't find my way to the depths. I started to panic. The reef was sharp, and the last thing I needed was to cut myself. I searched for Matt, but he was too far away. *I could become shark bait.* My stomach was only inches from the top of the coral as I desperately tried to regulate my breaths. *Stay calm.* The sea seemed to push me just when my body grazed the reef, and miraculously I had found deeper water. That was enough of an adrenaline rush for a while.

⁓

It wasn't long before Matt's family welcomed me into theirs. They visited regularly, so it was easy to get to know and feel comfortable with them. His parents lived in the house he grew up in, down the street and around the corner from his own.

I learned of the bushland Matt roamed when he was young, where he rode horses and dirt bikes for hours on end. A cycling circuit now took up some of that space, but much of the surrounding land had been preserved. A separate path ran next to the tidal creek, connecting to a major bikeway for many kilometers along the coast. I didn't know what a great thing this was until I followed it one day on Matt's bike.

For as close as we were to the city, and the traffic and development that delivered, five minutes on this route made me forget it. The creek was high with the tide, and I did a double-take as mullet flung themselves into the air, flashing silver before splashing back into the water. Nature was everywhere and became the soundtrack to the ride. Tiny birds like those in a storybook fluttered around the tops of wildflowers while the long grass in the wetlands waved in the breeze. The setting sun cast a dramatic blood-orange light that spilled across the sky, and the landscape flattened to shrubby bushes, then grew into dense mangroves.

I approached another field that from a distance, appeared to be full of lavender, similar to a scene in France. The wind was against me. A willie wagtail crossed in front of the bike, seemingly guarding this area, and I mimicked her song. Tinnies sped along the creek as it widened to the right, and I could hear golf balls being hit on the course ahead. A signed boardwalk indicated cyclists to the left, and as the bike tires rumbled over the loose wooden planks, I spotted a migrant bird foraging in the muddy scrub.

In the diminishing glow, there were all sorts of quietly active, inconspicuous spectators of the mud flats. The track went through a little patch of forest scattered with pine needles, and I instantly felt transported home. Just a short section on the road, then an open view of the glistening bay. I exhaled with gratitude for such an unforeseen discovery.

We were going on a fishing trip. On the way to the boat ramp, we passed through a small town filled with sugar cane fields, golden in the sunlight. "Those fields are definitely snake-infested," Matt said. My attention was drawn to a lonely-looking house on stilts, like a sitting duck amidst them. We pulled into the parking lot just down the road and got the boat ready. Peacocks strutted around the yard, their brilliant plumage on show for all to see.

The temperature was mild as we cruised along the channel to the bay, then to the chosen estuary. The midges came out in swarms when the sun set, comparable, if not worse than the black flies during springtime at home. Matt took out a bloodworm and baited a hook. When the last hint of color vanished from the sky, the bugs got so bad that I had to retreat to the cabin. I could hear Matt spray himself with insect repellant while he continued to fish in the dark. The night was long and I woke up often, hearing random taps on the sides of the boat, which to me were nudges by sharks.

As the first glimmer of dawn streamed through the mangroves, eagle calls broke into the placid morning and I sat up to see the birds as they glided across a palette of colors. Kookaburras erupted into laughter and cued my rise. Matt had already rigged a line and cast it into the water, precisely timing the tide's run out to catch some whiting. "Morning," I said.

"Hey, babe." He gave me a quick peck, his eyes remaining on the rod. It started to bend with force.

"It's a big one!"

"Probably just a ray." He pulled upward as the creature tried to ground himself.

He kept pulling and sure enough, a large stingray surfaced. All I could think of was Steve Irwin's freak accident. He cut the line and I watched him rig three more. *Tap tap. Tap tap tap.* It was on. All of the lines were getting successive bites, and soon we were reeling in whiting after whiting. "We have dinner sorted for tonight!" Matt said happily as he took the hook out of a fish and handed him to me. I paused to gently cradle his slick body between my palms. It was both confronting and humbling to catch our own food, and I secretly thanked all the fish we caught that day.

Australia was a place where I had fallen in love not only with the diversity of the land, but with this amazing man whom I had met so unexpectedly. I didn't know what our future would bring, but I felt that our time together was not over. I hugged Holly goodbye and she was her cheerful self, paying no attention to my luggage.

Matt sat with me at the airport, our eyes wet with tears. "I'll come and visit you at Christmas," he assured me. Boarding the plane now, I had mixed feelings. I had just experienced an adventure that far exceeded my expectations, surprising me with more than I could have imagined. But what would it be like when I went home? I had a different kind of love there… It was an entirely separate world.

CHAPTER FIVE:

The Visitor

There was nothing more exciting to me than going home to Cocoa. It was the most anticipated part of my return. I was about to witness a reaction that was so beautifully loving, I would feel forgiven for all the time I had been away.

As soon as I saw Mama's welcoming face, the brash arrival into Los Angeles after my unbelievable year abroad was erased from my thoughts. Country life in Andover was within reach. Passing all the familiar places on the way there, I could feel my heart pounding like a drum initiating a powerful ceremony. We were getting closer.

I marveled at the pine boughs on our road, heavy with fresh snow and dangling in the path of the jeep, brushing against it as we climbed the hill. At the head of the driveway, I was brimming with emotion. The front of the house came into view, and I caught a brief glimpse of Cocoa's dark face in my bedroom window, looking out at the approaching vehicle before disappearing. Mama parked and handed me the keys, nodding with a smile on her face and making no attempt to move from her seat.

In the dimness of the evening, I unlocked the front door and turned the knob. The predictable creak of the hinge invited me inside. "Cokie!" I cried as she half ran, half wiggled toward me. She tucked her nose at the base of my neck, licking my face, whimpering, then collapsing onto the floor. "I missed you so much!" I hugged her and sat to give her ear and tummy scratches, her eyes radiating warmth that I felt to my core. A tear of happiness trickled down my cheek, and I giggled to see another trickle on the floor as Cocoa rose up and went to the door. I opened it and raced out to chase her, and Mama knew we had our precious reunion.

Being home was surreal. It seemed like nothing had changed and everything had changed at the same time. Cocoa was full-grown now, her energy as abundant as I had known it to be. She was by my side once again, and I relished in her company. Not a day went by that wasn't devoid of loving attention. But there were instances when I caught her staring my way as if she had picked up on something imperceptible to me. I couldn't explain it other than how it made me feel sad.

Almost a month had gone by since my return, and Matt was coming to visit me and meet my family. I wished for everything to be wonderful during his stay. A white Christmas was promising as it was snowing again, the barren ground already hidden. I opened the door to see Cocoa standing there, a serious look on her face as she carried the weight of a snow carpet on her body. I laughed and grabbed a broom, lightly sweeping her off before she bounded indoors.

Mama and I planned to get a Christmas tree before Matt arrived. In past years, we had gone to the lot down the road. Now that it was no longer maintained, the evergreens crowded and overgrown, the nursery a few towns away was our next choice.

"Paw and my first tree was made from fallen pieces of pine boughs so that we could spare a tree. He drilled holes in the biggest branch and stuck the smaller branches into them, then we spent hours threading a cranberry and popcorn garland to decorate it," Mama said, her mind reliving the memory.

"Wow, that's really amazing." I imagined this sustainable simplicity. I liked it.

"Oh, we vowed never again. It was so tedious, but the love — the love we shared in those moments..." Her smile said it all.

The nursery had a huge selection of trees. "Jingle Bells" played, and feeling in the Christmas spirit, we combed the lot. "How about this one?" I pointed to a hardy pine that seemed to call out to me.

"Hmmm. I think we'd have to trim it too much to fit downstairs." Judging by the trees, it looked like no matter what, we'd have to alter the height. Then our eyes fell on the same one around the corner. "That's it!" Mama said. It was a perfectly full Balsam fir, not much taller than us. We lifted it into the jeep.

That night, classic Christmas carols blared downstairs as we decorated one of the most beautiful trees I had ever seen. Cocoa went over and drank from the stand before finding her spot under the lowest boughs where it was nice and cool. I joined her. "You're the best present we could ever receive," I said, combing my fingers through her soft hair.

Matt finally came down the escalator to the baggage claim in Logan Airport, standing out in his red jacket, tanned freckled skin, and dashing blond looks. I was love-struck. My heart fluttered as I ran toward him, his thick accent greeting me into his open arms. "Welcome to Boston!" I attempted the twangy pronunciation. As we waited outside for the shuttle to the hotel, the frigid wind blew through us, our breath exposed midair. "How cold is it, Matt?" He shivered.

"Freeeeezing!" His grin was infectious, and I hugged him tightly. It was incredible to have him on this side of the world, his presence the proof I needed that our experience together wasn't just an illusion.

The windchill dipped, and we resembled indistinguishable marshmallow people in our puffy coats, hats, and gloves, taking in the attractions of Boston. We happened upon a horse-drawn carriage with the coachman feeding the horses. "I'll be ready in five. Hop on in!" He motioned to the carriage and we climbed inside, covering up with a plush red blanket for further warmth. The horses began to trot, the bells on their halters jingling festively while snowflakes filled the air. It was as if we were in a fairytale.

On the bus to Concord, I became increasingly eager for Matt to see my childhood home, meet my family, and stay in rural New Hampshire. I had no doubt that everyone would like my Aussie boyfriend. Looking out the window, the snow drifts swept across the landscape, frosting the pines into seasonal glory. I could feel Matt's wonder and excitement for the newness of everything.

We waited briefly at the bus station before Mama walked in, grinning from ear to ear. After the phone chats, it was just the physical acquaintance now. "Hi, Matt! Welcome!" She extended her arms.

"Hi, Brendy, thanks! It's great to be here," he said as he hugged her.

"How was Boston? What do you think so far?"

"It was fun, about the same size as Brisbane. It's bloody cold, but I love it!"

"Well, I have the woodstoves roaring at home, so it'll be quite toasty!" Met by the blustery weather again, we loaded his luggage into the back and gratefully jumped into the heated vehicle. Mama treated us to some soup, bread, and chili at a main street café, and with our bellies full, we headed home. I couldn't wait for Matt to meet Cocoa. I wasn't sure he understood entirely how special she was to me.

It was spitting snow, turning into squalls against the windshield, and the conversation was cheery as we took in the decor of the season. Almost every front door displayed a pine wreath, and the big colonial houses had a traditional white taper candle in each window. Christmas trees were trimmed with an assortment of lights, and as carols played on the radio, it all seemed so enchanting.

The traffic ceased and the trees thickened upon reaching our road, now a tunnel of drooping pine boughs. The gray sky gave a glimpse of afternoon sunlight that made the snow sparkle. Seeing this through Matt's eyes made it all the more remarkable.

"I'll go and get Cocoa," I said when we arrived at the house. As I opened the door, she ran to me, her bum curling around, her tail bud wagging crazily as she showered me with kisses before falling to the floor. I would never tire of this greeting. It nourished my heart. A few hours, a day, a year... This was her same reaction. She made me feel so loved, so incredibly special every single time. "Cokie, there's someone here to meet you." She lifted her head and listened carefully, then went out to investigate.

When she saw Mama, her signature sway was in motion until Matt got out of the jeep, standing tall and strange. Her tone immediately changed, and she started jumping up and barking at him through a pursed mouth. "Hi, Cocoa!" he said with enthusiasm. He put his arms out to invite her closer, but she eyed him suspiciously, lowering her head with a growl.

"It's okay, girl." I gave him a hug to communicate that he wasn't anyone to fear. Still, she stood and watched from a distance, a perpetually disapproving look on her face.

As we made a move to bring in the luggage, she steered clear of Matt, her ears back and her tail bud down. I knelt to frame her face with my mitted hands and planted a kiss on her forehead. She remained wary, quickly moving out of his path as she continued to monitor him. I pushed the door open, and we were met with the tremendous warmth from the woodstove and the smell of freshly-baked banana bread.

"Welcome to our humble abode! You can put your stuff over there for now," Mama said, gesturing to the living room.

"Cocoa, c'mere!" Matt coaxed.

"Come on, girl," I called to her, but she just stared at me and turned to look at Matt cautiously, standing her ground.

"Better close the door, we're losing heat. She'll scratch when she wants to come in." Mama began to give Matt a tour of the house. "My husband and I moved to this area shortly after we eloped. It was part of his grandfather's land, and he offered it to us when he heard about our ideas of living simply. I don't think he ever believed we'd follow through with our plan. We would park at the foot of what started as an animal path, carrying all our supplies in. It was pretty rough, but the privacy in the wilderness was exactly what we dreamt of. We lived up here for five years before anyone in town found out."

She paused to get the tool to open the stovetop and added another log to the fire. Matt watched with interest as the flames were fed. Some wood smoke drifted out and hovered around the ceiling before the door squealed shut, snapping him out of his trance. He took off his jacket and unlaced his boots.

"You can put them under the stove. They'll dry there," Mama instructed before continuing. "We wanted to live as minimalists with little impact on the environment, so we built an eight by ten foot cabin that had no electricity or running water." She walked to the front door window and pointed at the structure partially hidden behind the tall snow banks. "That was it! Amaliya was our first-born, and we hung her bassinet from the ceiling so she would be warmer in the rising heat from the woodstove. We planned to have more children and knew we'd outgrow the cabin before long, so that's when we began the construction of this house."

There was a scratch at the door, and I quickly moved to open it. Cocoa walked in, finally surrendering to the cold, glaring over at Matt. I took a biscuit from the jar and put my fists down. "Choose." She pawed my hand and happily gobbled the biscuit, then moved sheepishly around Matt to find her spot under the kitchen table.

Mama brushed her fingers along a wall. "Everything in this house was built from materials we re-used from Jimmy's construction work — wood, barn boards, copper, mirrors... We had considered alternative means of energy efficiency and decided to use a solar glass façade as a passive heating and cooling system. The house faces southeast, so we get the morning sun streaming in until midday." Matt surveyed the space, taking in the details of a house with many stories.

Cocoa trailed us upstairs, still keeping a careful eye on the stranger. I took a seat on the piano bench and started playing while Mama and Matt found their places to watch the performance. Cocoa whimpered and broke into song, glancing at her audience, then moving closer to me as she hit the high notes with full-body bellows. We applauded her at the end, and she snuck a proud look at Matt before returning to one of skepticism.

"Now how about some banana bread?" Mama said. The heavenly smell had enticed us from the moment we arrived. Matt chose to sit in my usual seat at the table, so Cocoa moved to the farthest end. As soon as the bread was sliced, I felt her chin on my leg, and she nosed up at me. I broke a piece for her.

"Matt, try and give her a little," I suggested. He put his hand under the table. Cocoa turned to him guardedly, but seeing the offering, she quietly took it.

The night was very cold, and drafts came in through the weather-worn solar glass. Matt and I were tucked into my bed when Cocoa came up the stairs, the floorboards creaking in their usual spots from her weight. She stood outside my open door but didn't come any closer. "Come here, girl!" I said, petting the bed as an invitation. She walked toward me until she saw Matt's face and gave me a look of disgust before leaving us. "It's just a matter of time," I reassured him, switching off the lamp. *Clang, clang, thud.*

"What was that?" he asked. I laughed.

"Cocoa throws her bone down the stairs." I listened to her follow in pursuit. Mama's distant voice acknowledged her, and sounds of the woodstoves being loaded became background noise as I drifted off to sleep.

We parked at my father's home. I wasn't sure how Matt would react to meeting him. "Paw can't say anything, but you'll see that he speaks with his eyes," I said. Only a few of my friends had met him in his debilitated condition and had been uncomfortably quiet. I understood that for some, it was challenging to be in a one-way conversation. But by paying attention to body language, Paw was saying a lot, especially through his stunning blue eyes that lit up when he was engaged in communication.

We went inside and met the staff and housemates on the way to his bedroom. He was in his wheelchair, alert upon our approach. "Hi, Paw!" I said cheerfully, giving him a big hug. "This is Matt, my Australian boyfriend you've heard all about!" Matt smiled and moved in for a handshake, but quickly realizing my father couldn't voluntarily move his hand, he touched his palm instead. Paw nodded in greeting.

I told him about our adventures overseas — the climate, wildlife, boating, islands, and fishing, pausing every so often to have Matt clarify details. "I plan on moving there," I revealed. Paw lifted his head, surprised and concerned, searching my face for more information.

"I'll take care of her. You have my word," Matt promised him, stepping closer and putting his arm around my shoulder. Paw turned to study him. I hoped he was seeing the warmth and honesty that I did. He maintained eye contact for a minute before giving him a definitive nod of approval, and I exhaled with relief.

"We need some tunes in here," I said, finding our favorite song by Bonnie Raitt. When he could willingly move his arms, Paw would play an air guitar as I belted out the lyrics. Even today, in my mind and in his eyes, he was still accompanying me. The music filled the corners of the room. I let it play on and positioned his wheelchair so he faced the window to see the birds on the feeder. Lingering in the doorway for a minute after saying goodbye, I wondered what his thoughts were as he gazed outside.

In the jeep, Matt was silent for a while. Finally, he spoke. "Are you sure you want to move to Australia? You'd be leaving everyone, and I can see how much they mean to you." There was a degree of hesitancy in his voice, and I could tell that meeting my father had really affected him.

"I am sure." I was confident and strong, maybe because I was home and couldn't separate myself from the present connectedness. "I love everyone, but it's my life and my choice. I want to be with you no matter where you are."

"Then you'll have to visit them regularly," he said, squeezing my hand.

Throughout our stay at home, Matt and I frequently awoke to Mama loading the woodstoves. This time, it was almost midnight. "I think your mum's a firebug!" he whispered. I giggled. The stoves had to be fed every few hours or else the house's temperature would quickly drop. I took the next shift and got up quietly. The house was completely dark aside from the sliver of light that shone through the flywheel of the upstairs woodstove. I knew the house by heart — every floorboard, every stair, every wall.

There were decent coals left in the downstairs woodstove. I loaded it to the top again, closing it quickly so not to smoke up the house. Cocoa was sprawled out on one of the couches and I knelt over to kiss her cheek, smoothing down her coat before returning to my room. Matt was awake. "I think you're a firebug too!" he said in a funny little voice that made me laugh.

Only once did he attempt to navigate the house in the dark. His heavy steps were like elephant feet hitting every creak. I drifted off to sleep until he climbed back into bed. "I missed the last stair and Cocoa was at the bottom," he said. "She nearly attacked me!" From that night on, Matt used a flashlight when he got up. And oftentimes, I heard him load the woodstoves. *Firebug*, I thought to myself.

Christmas was spent in the woods with all of our traditional festivities. On Christmas Eve, my sister Amaliya, her husband, Crayton, Katie and her boyfriend, Mike, joined us. Amaliya sliced crosses into chestnuts and put them on the stovetop to roast, and when their shells started to curl, we burned our fingers trying to get into their sweet nuttiness too soon. Matt tasted his first glass of eggnog, then spiked it with Bundaberg Rum. The radio was set to play the annual broadcast of *A Christmas Carol* just as Ben, with his signature DJ voice, announced it on-air. The crotchety old man Ebenezer Scrooge spoke out as the story began. Cocoa lay under the table and I rubbed her soft coat with my feet.

The Christmas tree stood pleasantly in the living room. White lights adorned the needled branches with ornaments old and new, gift boxes were already set around the trunk, and the fragrant pine smell filled the air. The wooden manger James built displayed the nativity scene, which included Amaliya's quirky addition of a "shepherd" troll with a tissue head mantle. Candles flickered, the stockings hung upstairs, and there was much goodwill and cheer.

Katie and I marveled at the presents, easily giving in to the nostalgia of our childhood. We each chose one to unwrap, and Cocoa took interest. "I know you have some here, Cokie." She tilted her head as I rummaged through the pile and placed a tightly wrapped bundle near her. She put a paw on it, tearing the paper with her teeth and swiftly discarding it to the side. A large ball broke free. She nudged it for a moment, then stared at us. Her present was good, but it was obvious she liked unwrapping better.

Mama closed the door, returning from the shed with a few pieces of wood, a look of concern on her face. "It's pretty slippery out there," she said. The sun had melted the fresh snow on the driveway, and it was now frozen into glare ice. "I put ash in the front and that's helped, but the hill…" There was no way the rest of the family, especially Paw traveling in the accessible van, would be able to get up the road.

"We can ash it," I said, looking to Matt, Katie, and Mike in agreement. The guys lifted the black barrel of stored stove ash into the back of the jeep and propped it outward. The four of us worked together in the frigid temperature, driving slowly and scooping out ash along the road, our clothes filthy but our spirits high. We got the job done in the quiet darkness, then gratefully welcomed the heat from the woodstoves. The carols could be heard all around the house that night.

I woke up early and tiptoed downstairs. Cocoa was resting by the Christmas tree with a blanket spread out on her, and I crouched down for a hug. She stretched and got up. I couldn't help but laugh as she walked to Mama's room still draped with the blanket. She fixated on the resting body, and a hand reached out in greeting, not quite ready to get up. Still, Cocoa waited, edging a little closer. "It's just Mama!" I whispered as she nosed toward her face. My mother's eyes popped open and looked from me to Cocoa, who joyfully lapped her cheek. What a way to begin the holiday.

It was a full house with the addition of Paw and my grandmother, Nana, James and his wife, Lauren, and Ben and his fiancé, Christina. The woodstoves roared, music played, and warmth and laughter filled the rustic home. I glanced at Matt, who seemed to relish in it. He had a big dimpled smile on his face as he followed the cheerful conversation around the living room.

Almost everyone had trouble understanding his thick accent riddled with Australian slang. I remembered how difficult it had been for me, especially on the phone. I listened carefully to discern details and guessed my responses. Now I watched everyone with amusement as they stared at Matt, trying to figure out what he said, their eyes lighting up in recognition as they caught on and repeated their interpretations. Mama grinned, nodded, and laughed like she understood until I translated.

Cocoa had unwrapped her presents, eager for treats, and made her rounds to everyone except Matt before standing at the door. As much as she loved the company of extended family, with it came prolonged loudness and too much to monitor, which made her very anxious. I let her outside and watched as she plunged her nose into the snow and ate it, then began to roam the yard. I couldn't resist the setting and joined her. The sun glowed through the gray sky while snowflakes fell silently. I smiled. The afternoon had just a little bit of Christmas magic about it.

The few weeks of Matt's visit were spent with my family, at home in the woods, and touring around on our own. He had a lot in common with my siblings, which was probably why he was accepted like a brother or childhood friend. That rapport carried over to my parents. It was amazing to watch the fun-loving bond he instantly shared with Mama. "You're just like her," he said. I knew I wasn't as patient and kind, but I smiled at his compliment. He was deeply respectful to Paw, and that meant a lot to me. Just by the way he interacted with my family, I could clearly see him becoming a permanent part of my life.

He was like a little boy in a winter wonderland, capturing photos everywhere we went. He zoomed in on my favorite chickadees, incredibly resilient through the freezing weather, chirping loudly, announcing their existence. One day as we drove along, Matt frantically pointed out the window. "A small creature running! Pull over, look!" My eyes found what he was so enthusiastic about, and I started giggling at his unfamiliarity.

"That's a red squirrel."

"A squirr-EL," he enunciated. I smirked.

"I love their long tails. And wait until you see chipmunks. They'll speak their mind to anyone!" I thought of them telling off bears in the woods as they disputed their share of forage. It really was so refreshing to see this world through Matt's eyes. Even what was deemed common to locals was interesting to him.

We went down to the pond, discovering rabbit, deer, turkey, moose, and coydog tracks, then trekked through the snowy paths in the woods. Walking on the frozen lake in town, little air pockets cracked loudly around the perimeter every few steps. Matt watched with astonishment as a fisherman drove his truck across the ice to a bob house. He quickly took to the small-town way of life, driving on the country roads, shoveling snow for the first time, bringing in wheelbarrows of wood, and building fires.

The windchill plummeted to a new low on the same day we planned to go skiing. As snow drifts blew across the road and the local radio announcer gave a bleak weather forecast, we braved it out. Matt had bought us winter gear for Christmas, so thankfully, we had balaclavas and all the outer and underwear to buffer us. But after a couple runs, the bitter cold seeped into our bodies. We took on a whole new appreciation for hot chocolate as we warmed up in the ski lodge that afternoon.

The extreme conditions persisted as we boarded the Amtrak headed to New York City. Speeding by small towns along the way, this pace continued. We jumped on and off tour buses — seeing the attractions, getting quick photos, then conceding to the weather, finding refuge in the warm restaurants of Little Italy. Matt met Abby, my good friend from high school. She told me she had never seen me as happy as I seemed with him. It was helpful to hear her perspective because everything was happening so fast.

Everyone liked Matt except for Cocoa, who kept a watchful eye on him. The only time she would go near him was when he bribed her with food. Regardless of his efforts to pat her or get close in any other way, she hastily moved out of his reach.

I wanted her to love him, to show him the same affection she gave me, and be willing to receive his warmth in return. Was she jealous he was getting more of my attention? Or was it merely a result of her distrust of strangers? She had no real forewarning of this male guest, so maybe it was the abrupt invasion of her space. Toward the end of his visit, I caught her staring at the two of us interacting. It seemed like she was beginning to understand our connection.

As I said goodbye to Matt, it was clear that he was enraptured by my home, my family, and such a simple lifestyle embracing nature. He was so relaxed with all of it. We would surely find a way to be together again, maybe through another visa. I was suddenly faced with the reality that I had to make major decisions.

CHAPTER SIX:

Heart and Heartbreak

Cocoa followed me upstairs and stopped at the piano, lifting her head over the bench to stare at the keys. I smiled. "Mama's asleep, Cokie. I'll play it in the morning, okay?" She gave me a perturbed look but proceeded into my room and jumped onto the bed to find her position at the window.

The front yard was cloaked in moonlight, and I took my place next to her as she peered out, sniffing the air and waiting patiently. She rested her chin on the windowsill, her little patch of white hair hidden from view. As lightning bugs flickered randomly in the peaceful night, I scanned the yard to see how many I could spot, then rested my chin like Cocoa, watching and waiting. The peepers were in full harmony and a whippoorwill took the lead.

A lone coydog pierced the meditative song with a few yips and a howl, calling in his pack. Cocoa's deep growl erupted into a ferocious bark as she jumped off the bed and went to the door. "No, Cokie, you can't go out, it's too dangerous!" I said. She looked at me with pleading eyes, but knew I meant business. I could be just as protective.

Loud yips and howls from the forming pack sent her into territorial panic and she sprung against the door, her body pulsating with her aggressive tone. I heard Mama get up. "Don't let her out, the coydogs are running!" she called from the bottom of the stairs.

"Don't worry, I won't!" I said.

"The full moon's calling to them." It was an exceptional night for the wild things in the woods. Hearing Mama, Cocoa went to the top of the stairs, inevitably wanting a different outcome. "No, Cokie, you have to stay in," Mama told her sternly.

"Come on, girl!" I said, grabbing a book off the shelf in an effort to calm her. The *Frog and Toad* stories were the best because I could use Mr. Froggy to narrate them. She loved it, tilting her head when I moved him around dramatically. Those books were downstairs, so tonight it would be *The Little Mouse, The Red Ripe Strawberry, and The Big Hungry Bear.* Cocoa bounded up next to me, poised at the window as I started reading.

Everything became quiet, but she was restless and jumped onto the floor, disappearing into the living room and returning with an old marrow bone hanging out of her mouth. She stared at me before reclaiming her spot on the bed. I continued reading to the noise of her knocking the bone against her teeth as she wore it down. "Now that's one red, ripe strawberry the big, hungry Cocoa Bear will never get — except when Mandy decides to share it with her!" I kissed her nose and closed the book. Lights out. But in the perfectly clear night sky, the moon shone on.

Cocoa let her bone fall to the floor and resumed guard duty. Just as I began to doze off, I heard a branch breaking near the old outhouse. My guardian was breathing heavily in a deep sleep and missed it. I fumbled for my glasses. Across the front lawn was a big black bear lumbering toward the house. I loved watching these intriguing animals, and my eyes were glued to him as he approached the bird feeder. The peaceful sighting was cut short when Cocoa awoke in a fit of frenzy. With tremendous speed and agility, the bear bolted up the tree only feet from my window.

It took all my strength to prevent Cocoa's strong body from going through the screen. She finally leapt off my bed, demanding to be let outside. Despite her persistent barking, the bear soon realized she was a contained threat. I watched him dangle one limb then another as he found the ground and took off into the woods. The sound of sticks breaking gave away his escape route. Cocoa was on my bed again, protesting his flight and putting out a warning to others daring to trespass. With all the excitement this time, it took a while for both of us to settle into sleep. I lay there with my favorite cuddle buddy twitching her paws as she undoubtedly dreamt of her wild bear chase.

Matt's parents had generously offered to fly me to Brisbane for my birthday. Cocoa took notice right when I began to pack. She rested her chin on her paws and looked up at me through sad yellow eyes, making me feel every guilty chord in my heart. "It's okay, girl," I said gently, "I'll be back." I sat on the floor to hug her, but she remained still. Maybe I should have organized my bags in more of a stealthy manner to minimize her upset.

Despite the tears that rolled down my cheeks, it was easier leaving now because I knew I would return in a couple of weeks. I kissed Cocoa and gave her a biscuit, then quickly hid a few under the pillows on the couches. "Bye, Cokie, I love you. See you soon." She held my gaze before going into the living room and I closed the door, focusing on the road ahead. It had been three months since Matt's visit, and I wondered if things would be the same between us.

The flight was as long as ever but with a definitive result — having someone to go to rather than setting forth on my own. In Brisbane, I ducked into the bathroom to make my disheveled appearance presentable, then proceeded through customs and waited while my maple syrup was inspected and cleared. When I entered the lobby, I caught my Aussie bloke's eye in the crowd, and he strode toward me. Even though we had communicated via Skype, it was like we were seeing each other for the first time. I couldn't help but giggle.

The weather was pleasantly warm with a faithfully cloudless sky. As Matt pulled the ute into the driveway, Holly welcomed it. "Wait here," he said, "see if she detects anything." I smiled as he got out and greeted her. She pranced over to him with a ball, but dropped it quickly when he lifted my luggage from the back tray. I opened the door.

"Holly!" I cried. She let out a bark of delight and ran to me. I hugged her for the few seconds she allowed and smoothed down her coat, her frame noticeably small in comparison to Cocoa's. She raced by us, up the side ramp and into the house, her long tail wagging freely while her mouth was wide with a border collie smile. She was indeed used to being inside, and it was consoling to think she and Matt were in each other's company when I was home.

Matt had booked a weekend away on the beautiful Sunshine Coast, and we arrived on another picturesque Queensland day. Our unit looked out at the ocean, sparkling as if thousands of fireflies were dancing on the water's surface. My eyes were entranced by it. We strolled along the boardwalk amidst mangroves, taking in the salty breeze and relaxing in seaside bliss.

While I got ready for our dinner out, Matt scrolled through the iPod, trying to decide on some music. "Do you want to listen to this?" It sounded good. I checked myself in the mirror just as an ice cube hit his scotch glass.

"The reservation's for six," I said, joining him in the living room.

"No need to rush." He offered me his hands and pulled me close for a slow dance as the romantic music serenaded us. I nestled into his arms, listening to the meaningful words until he let go of my side and swept his hand in front of me to reveal a ring.

"Mandy, will you marry me?" he asked confidently. I was so surprised. Only earlier we were talking about the visa process so we could be together, maybe get married down the line… He was so nonchalant, I had no idea he had already gotten a ring and planned the proposal. His words echoed in my ears, and I stared at his smiling face before realizing I hadn't responded.

"Yes! Definitely!" I threw my arms around him, and he swung me in the air. I was in awe of all that was unfolding. A glimpse of the future filled me with hope that I had found the person to spend my lifetime with.

The rest of my trip was full of celebration for our engagement and my twenty-seventh birthday. I couldn't take my eyes off the shiny gems that adorned my ring finger and the way the light reflected them, casting kaleidoscopic prisms everywhere. I replayed Matt's proposal in my head, his bright eyes when I agreed to marry him. Had I been destined to return to Australia for this very reason?

Following such a significant event, I settled back into living in the woods. Part of me knew I needed to soak up as much of the environment as possible before making the permanent move overseas. I found a work-from-home job to maximize the time I had left, especially with Cocoa. I couldn't yet come to terms with the thought of leaving her again.

I had heard of the waterfall. Paw used to take my brothers fishing there when he was well. All I imagined was rainbow light around a magnificent plumage of water spraying off a cliff of smooth rocks. Katie and I went part of the way along the brook when we were younger, back when Lady was alive. It seemed like an elusive destination to us as we were small and the journey appeared epic. Now the time had come for this adventure, and we went out the door with all of daylight ahead of us.

Cocoa stopped to check on me as we walked the familiar road that would eventually lead us on a new course. I jogged toward her and she bolted, swiftly circling the trees before returning to me, the extent of her tongue hanging out as she panted loudly. Suddenly, there were branches breaking nearby, and we turned in the direction of the sound. Cocoa's nostrils quivered in the air. The noise stopped. I strained to see through the foliage and could just make out a doe standing gracefully, peering at us.

There was more movement and another deer emerged. Cocoa had waited long enough and took off after them. Their white tails flipped up as they effortlessly leapt farther into the woods and disappeared. My pup doubled back with boundless energy, her tail bud wiggling. She dragged a large stick from the side of the unmaintained road and gave me my cue. "Rahrrr!" I rushed at her and grabbed the end. Neither of us let go of it as we ran together.

We reached the forested path where the great Snowy Owl had once lived. He was incredibly bewitching, with bright yellow eyes that commanded attention and explanation for our disturbance of his peaceful habitat. He looked down at Lady as she walked past his home amongst the tall pines, and I made eye contact with him, respectfully asking if we could pass. After a few seconds of seeming consideration, he stretched his broad wingspan and crossed above us to the pine boughs on the opposite side, out of sight, the invisible boundary lifted.

Today, there was a definite presence in this patch of woods. The owl was nowhere to be seen, yet it was as if we were still being observed. I stopped and tilted my head upward, fixated on the spots of clear blue sky glinting through the upper canopy of pine needles. I spun in a circle, stretching my arms out, and danced with the breeze. Cocoa barked happily and found her way down the hill by a small cabin near the edge of the pond. I followed her, briefly imagining that it was our place set upon this tranquil site by the water and the Snowy Owl's former domain.

Cocoa splashed about, and I looked over to see her blowing nose bubbles again. Her coat was clinging to her, showing off a now curvaceous form supported by long legs, her ears spikey with wispy strands of saturated hair. Her eyes were wild as I reached for a rock. She charged out of the water toward me, her strong front legs planted into the ground, ordering the game.

"Ready?" I tossed it above her and into the water. She made a move to chase it before realizing it was gone and turned back to me for more. I quickly fumbled around to collect a handful. Her high-pitched bark echoed across the pond as I whipped the rocks one by one. "Okay, Cokie, that's it!" I brushed my hands together. Game over. A sip from my water bottle, then I tossed a biscuit in the air, precisely met by my eager companion as she jumped up and caught it. "Let's go!" I sang. And like a fuzzy brown bear, she bounded up the hill.

As we neared the crossing of the main road to the path along Mountain Brook, the earth was waterlogged, the pond swollen from the recent wet weather. Careful not to soak my shoes, I balanced on branch debris and rocks to avoid the deep parts. Cocoa stormed right through, and I couldn't help but laugh. She was a muddy mess and didn't have a care in the world.

From the boulder blockade of the trail entrance, everything was new to Cocoa. She ran ahead, tracing an assortment of musky scents. How I wished I could identify what she could. With determined speed, we went up the pine path that eased back to the bubbling brook. Finding the closest access, Cocoa merrily waded into its depth. I steadied myself on a rock and tested the temperature. It was ice cold. Still, Cocoa lapped it up before competing with the weight of her drenched body and the current to return to the beaten path. She sprinted forward, stopping abruptly to shake off, refreshed and alert.

The sound of the rushing water became distant as the path wound up through a hardwood forest. Cocoa led confidently, pausing to smell some lowbush blueberries. A single strand of spider web stuck to my face as we walked through a narrow stretch, and I quickly brushed it off. In front of us loomed deep, dark, rocky landscape. I was filled with nervous excitement as Cocoa stopped and looked at me worriedly. This was as far as I had ever gone, and I was ready to step into the unknown.

The path was muddy, and the densely-wooded surroundings created a cool and shady environment. The brook could be heard again, but when it came into view, my momentarily apprehensive pup stayed by my side. I knew we were not alone, especially in this section. Eyes were on us, yet

I felt protected. Cocoa jumped up a couple of times, trying to dissuade me from moving forward.

"Cokie, it's okay, we're going to the waterfall! Come on!" I tried to reassure her. There was no avoiding the mud at this point. My legs were speckled and my shoes were brown. I balanced on a fallen tree, walking the length before hopping down and continuing on the rocky path. Cocoa was happy once more as we rounded the corner and the brook became completely accessible. She plunged in, rejoicing with her bubbles.

I sat cross-legged on a mossy boulder nearby. The sun radiated through and I looked upstream to see it glittering on the water. I was enthralled. This place was so peaceful, dreamy, wild... Something moved in the woods across the way and I waited, hoping its identity would be revealed. With a scuffle and a squabble, two gray squirrels raced about in the leafy undergrowth, one running up a birch tree while the other followed close behind.

Cocoa raised her nose out of the water and a stream of droplets dribbled from her chin as she looked toward the commotion. She jumped onto the banking and broke into a super-speed run, dodging trees, exposed roots, rocks, and mud puddles, moving with precision through the natural challenge course. I could feel her oozing happiness and felt the same way. Being immersed in nature on this adventure with Cocoa, all my anxieties, inhibitions, and doubts meandering downstream, I was in harmony with everything. I skipped along, singing and twirling.

I could hear the water strengthening in volume and there was brightness ahead. A field opened up to the right, and a bridge constructed of tree limbs and rope stretched above the brook on the left. I had heard of this bridge, perhaps another fishing story from the boys. It appeared too unsteady to cross now, with gaps where the wood had fallen out of its form.

I stayed on the main path, and the brook snaked around out of reach as the ground under my feet angled upward. Rocky caverns within the steep embankment offered perfect hideaway homes for many creatures. How active it would all be at night. The path diverged, and Cocoa chose the one closer to the brook. There was a gradual decline as the trees thinned out, and the power of the surge made it obvious — we had finally reached the legendary waterfall!

The white water cascaded over a rocky façade, splashing with incredible force into a deep pool below. The sound of it drowned out everything else until I spoke. "Cokie, let's go closer!" Her ears perked up, and knowingly, she navigated the descent. The brook separated from the pool, splitting to the sides of a small island that faced the waterfall. I jumped onto rocks to avoid getting wet, while Cocoa charged right through.

A fireplace and rock chairs were indications of the camping area. I pictured myself toasting marshmallows there, the strange sounds past the crackling fire filling me with wonder and fear of what lurked in the shadows. Cocoa went to sniff some charcoal remnants as I stared up at the waterfall. The sun cast its warmth on my face, soaking into my skin, and I closed my eyes. When I opened them, my gaze caught a multitude of colors splaying from the mist of the falling water. It was the very rainbow I had imagined.

I took off my shoes and peeled the muddy, wet socks from my skin, tapping at the water with my toes before slowly submerging both feet into its frigidity. Cocoa was done scoping out the land and waded into the pool, swimming to the center before paddling to me. "Don't do it!" I caught her mischievous eye as she rolled her head back and forth. I put my hands out to shield myself, but it was too late.

The icy water drops were shaken from her coat and onto me. I laughed and grabbed her face, scrunched up her mane, and kissed her nose. "Thank you, Cokie," I said. "This has been such an amazing experience with you!" The omniscient look she gave me in response confirmed that I was meant to share this journey with her. After all, she was my guide.

"Remember when I was young and had the atlas open and asked you where you'd like to go?" I said to Mama as we walked the well-trodden road one afternoon.

"Oh, yes."

"You said 'Australia.' " She nodded in recollection. "How funny that I am moving there, and surely one day you will visit!" I got lost in the vision of sharing all the picturesque scenes of the vast countryside with her before returning to the present. "Mama, you've done so much for me, always encouraged my independence and sense of adventure... I can't thank you enough!"

My wonderful mother smiled, modestly accepting the praise. I thought back to my struggles with self-confidence throughout the years. She was constantly there, wiping my tears away, helping me to understand and appreciate my own gifts, never once making me feel like I wasn't special. She was my figure of inspiration, my rock, truly shaping me in extraordinary ways.

I had no doubt that she did her very best to raise our family. Through turbulent times as my father battled illness, she selflessly soldiered on, becoming an advocate for his needs, all the while supporting five children. A woman of great faith and a pillar of strength, she held it together for us — instilling hope, trust, and optimism. Decades later, she remained a continual blessing in my life.

I could see Cocoa from my bedroom window, lying on the damp earth close to the woodshed. She was monitoring the yard with sophistication, her paws crossed in the way of a proper lady. "Cokie!" My eyes met hers, but she made no point to move until I opened the upstairs door and headed outside. Now I had her full attention. I perched on the big rock near the hemlock tree that had fallen when I was a child, which in my mind was home to mystical beings. The surface of the rock was carpeted with various green mosses, velvety as I brushed my hand over them.

Cocoa sat next to me, touching her nose to the moss, exhaling in a single spurt as if a bug had crawled into her nostril. The woods were abuzz with life. I felt peace and climbed off the rock to do pirouettes across the grass, singing out happily. Cocoa jumped up toward me to share in the merriment. "Let's go down to the well house!" I said, running past the cabin and around the back of the garden to escape the tangled thorns at the top of the hill. I could hear something heavy-footed move in the distance.

I looked in the direction of what used to be an immense pine forest with trees so tall, it was like a giant's territory. A wide pine needle path wound through it, with chunky roots posing as hurdles. The terrain sloped upward by a small pet cemetery, then led to the Black Forest, aptly named for its thick pines and hardwoods, their aged trunks filled with mysterious noises.

I remembered finding out that all of this would be clear-cut, unaware that it was my great-grandfather's decision. My siblings and I put notes on the excavators' vehicles, desperately hoping they would cease, but they didn't. I cried for days as the trees fell, the true value of them demolished in a tiny fraction of the time it took for them to grow. How I had loved that forest. I wished so much for it to be restored.

Cocoa seemed to be reading my thoughts, and as if to distract me from them, she wandered to an animal path. I followed her through shady patches and found a field where deer beds compressed the ivy groundcover. I pictured a herd cautiously resting, attentive and watchful of predators in the night. At least this place remained a haven for wildlife.

Cocoa stopped at the blueberry bushes in the field. I was thankful for the exceptionally snowy winter as their yield was plentiful. I filled my hand with the tiny lowbush treats while Cocoa ate freely, making a snuffing sound as she gorged on them like a bear. The balmy breeze blew scents of pure fruitiness from the strawberries and the fresh grass near the road to the pond. A change in direction and another note of heavenly perfume lingered on the exhale of the wind.

"Look, Cocoa!" I said, spotting a huge patch of pink roses growing amidst blackberry bushes and thorns. Maybe the elements were responsible for the spread, or perhaps a bird had dropped seeds from a garden. I stood there admiring the flowers, touching their silky petals, but I didn't pick them. They were too beautiful and random to disturb and should keep growing in this manner, a blissful discovery for passersby.

The sky was overcast as I stood on the dock, staring out at the pond. I challenged myself with the idea of jumping in, and the water seemed to darken. It daunted me, my imagination creating all kinds of creatures lurking in the depths, just waiting to reach out and grab me. Cocoa was by my side, peering into the water. I walked to the banking at the shoreline and found a stick for her, tossed it out, and she charged in without hesitation. She gave me courage as she had no fear at all.

I ran to the end of the dock. One... Two... THREE! My feet were stuck. I couldn't do it. *Come on, Amanda. Conquer it.* Cocoa approached the stick and grabbed it in her jaws, holding it tightly and looking up as she swam in a circle. It was as if she was waiting for me to choose the right moment to join her. One... Two... I closed my eyes, and as fear crippled my body, it was too late. I had already jumped in the air, plunging deep into the surprisingly cold water. Cocoa was swimming my way when I rose to the surface. "Cokie! I did it!" I cried, wiping my eyes as I treaded water. "Woohoooo!" my voice echoed across the pond.

She circled my body, her strong legs paddling with ease as she herded me toward the beach. In her company, I felt safe. Protected. We got to the shore and she clearly wanted to continue swimming, letting go of the stick for me to throw again. I ran onto the dock. Without thinking, I jumped high and dunked in, the water swirling around me, flushing my being. Cocoa and I were out deep with no one else, and I was light and burden-free.

I could smell the sweet rain before it started falling. It came down gently but thoroughly, covering the pond in one big sheet. I ran onto the dock and stood there, the drops blanketing me. "Wheeeeee!" I looked at what appeared to be a solid surface, a visual deception, and when I broke through it, I was encapsulated in the womb of nature.

As it became torrential, Cocoa and I sought refuge in the boathouse. I sat on the bench, gazing out at the water now devoid of darkness. In the midst of the summer afternoon, it was bright white with the downpour. So pure, misty, magical... It wasn't scary to me any longer, and I had my best friend, my dear guardian, to thank.

⁓

Pang! An acorn hit the kindling box outside and woke me from my slumber. I looked out to the sunny fall morning. Cocoa hurried around the yard, picking up on scents left behind by the visiting nocturnal animals. The leaves of the season were reaching their peak in color. I found myself staring at a large yellow one on the maple tree my parents had planted so many years ago as a struggling sapling.

The sun shone through the leaf, and I could just distinguish the veins highlighted with a touch of chlorophyll, green and vibrant. My mind was quiet as I took in the ever-changing scene. The birds chattered as they celebrated the wealth of seed from the feeder, and a red squirrel feasted on the fallen remnants. I watched as Cocoa made her way to the pile. The squirrel let out a cry of dismay and scampered off, leaving her to nibble on the seed hulls.

A loud gunshot rang out, creating momentary chaos in the surrounding woods. The start of hunting season. I cringed at the thought. Another gunshot. I imagined all the hunted animals taking refuge in our woods, safe from the unfair advantage hunters had over them with their specialized equipment.

Our neighbor was an avid hunter, and I had seen many of his trophy catches. His proud conquests were mounted, their beautiful faces and hides displayed, their marble eyes empty of the wild lives they once had. It broke my heart. I had great respect for these animals and held them sacred for they represented something so much more. I counted it a gift every time I saw these majestic beings in their habitat.

Mama was at the table, reading an even thicker novel than the last while holding the handle to her cup of tea. Cocoa rushed toward me, and I crouched to wrap my arms around her as she showered me with kisses. "Morning, Cokie, morning, Mummy." We spoke of our upset over the gunshots, and Cocoa stared at me as if sensing my sadness.

I knelt to hug her again. She stayed there, offering her compassionate presence as she simply let herself be held. Her hugs were the most comforting. She exuded such warmth, it was like she healed me of any woe, waiting for as long as I needed to hug her, never pulling away. I felt so loved and understood. When I got up, she wove through my legs and stopped for a bum scratch.

Today was Saturday, "Dump Day." I helped Mama gather the trash and recyclables, loaded the jeep, and all of us piled in. Cocoa straddled the foot space, her hind legs on the back seat and front paws balanced on the small center console between the front seats. "Where are we going, Cokie?" I asked. Her ears perked up as her tail bud wiggled. She knew this weekly routine very well.

Driving down the roads into town, the season exhibited itself vividly. First in the hills and valleys of Ragged Mountain, visible from the foot of our dirt road. People were outside raking, stacking wood, and fixing their yards in preparation for the upcoming winter months. I watched some kids jump into a leaf pile and smiled, thinking about the previous weekend when I had done just that.

I had been combing the earth with a rake, gathering a bounty of dulling leaves that had fallen in their glory. The cleared patch was damp, cool ground under the stairs, and Cocoa immediately settled onto it. I formed a towering pile of leaves and my inner child took over. I laughed and threw myself in. Cocoa bounded up, plowing into the leaves after me while barking excitedly, her voice cracking into happy soprano notes.

Now at the landfill, she hung her head out the window. As Mama and I discarded the bags, I noticed the shed attendant walk to the jeep window where Cocoa was. With her distrust of strangers, I listened for her ferocious bark, but as I watched closely, she took the biscuit the woman offered her without a sound. I smiled. "She does that every time," Mama told me.

Cocoa licked my face, then repeated the affectionate gesture with Mama. "You're so special, Cokie," I said. We pulled into the bank drive-through, and she peered out the window expectantly. When the teller returned the transaction drawer, I saw why — two little biscuits sat on top of the account receipt. No wonder she loved the Saturday morning routine!

On the speed strip toward the east side of town, Cocoa faced the wind, closing her eyes as it forcibly blew her mouth into a gaping smile. Dogs were obviously known for loving this, and I wanted to see what it was like. Mama grinned at me and pressed down the button on the defunct electronics to open my window.

I tilted my head out and closed my eyes as I was greeted by a strong gust. The crisp air felt invigorating and made the straggling baby hairs on my forehead flutter about. The smell of wood fires was everywhere. My entire face went tingly, my cheeks blushed with color, my ears deafened by the wind. I moved back into the vehicle feeling refreshed.

Mama went inside the post office, and I looked at the backseat passenger. Her brilliant eyes gleamed with pure joy as she waited. What an immense presence she had. Her tail bud started wiggling as the building's door opened and Mama walked out, waving yet another biscuit in the air.

I sat at the table one night, compiling the visa documentation. There were many details to organize. I was lost in thought until I tuned into a scuffling near the living room. My eyes scanned the area. In the dim light to the left of the hutch was Cocoa's face. Her wispy ear hair frizzed out, giving her the appearance of a lion, her eyes tawny and wide, focused on me as she stood still on the upper stairs.

I held her gaze until she headed down, and I quickly hid behind the wooden post. She walked cautiously toward my hiding spot, stopping a few feet in front of me. I popped out and she jumped. "It's just me, Cokie, it's *just me!*" I cried. She wiggled and waggled, burying her face in my arms, her coat smelling like gingerbread cookies.

It was September — a perfect time to go up to the field and see if any wildflowers remained. How I enjoyed them! The tiger lilies, so vivid with their burnt-orange color, and the sunflowers, happy beings in salutation. The various purple, pink, and white blossoms sporadically strewn by the wind, then the creamy white milkweeds that were silk decadence to my skin.

I opened the door to see Cocoa standing in the front yard, ready for another adventure. Pinching a little biscuit from my pocket, I tossed it to her, and we were off. Despite the cooler temperature, there was a pleasant undertone of warmth and my body felt light as we walked up the driveway. Cocoa raced ahead, grabbing a stick and giving me the eye to chase her. "I'm gonna get you!" I waved my arms and ran after her until I reached the birch tree with the scar from where I had peeled off a strip of bark for a childhood art project. I placed my hand on the darkened layer, gently apologizing to the tree for hurting it.

Cocoa picked up a scent. I followed her, moving around mud tracks that were partially covered with seasonal leaves. Some flaunted such magnificence that I bent down to collect them. Cocoa was right there expecting acorns, and as they were abundant, I quickly filled my hand. "Back it up!" I motioned, and she let out a shrill squeal of delight that changed the meditative energy of the morning. She caught the first one in her mouth, chewed, and dropped it. Staggering her stance, she impatiently waited for me to throw the next ones until there was rustling in the leaves nearby. She paused, looking in its direction.

The sun cast spider-like diamonds through the pine trees, and I wished I had my camera. Trying to capture this beauty in my memory, I walked slowly in the middle of the narrow road. Cocoa moved to the base of a tree and stuck her nose into the leaves, catching a scent once again. She raised her sight line to the woods while I stared at the fallen oak to my left, now mossy and teeming with new life.

Just before the field, Cocoa tried to herd me backward. "It's okay, girl," I told her. I walked over the downed wire that had once warded off trespassers and traipsed on the bent grass of an animal trail. The only flowers I saw were some Indian paintbrush that caught my attention amongst the dwindling vegetation. Milkweeds stood broken open, empty, or dried. I found one with a few silky hairs left inside and pulled them out, brushing their softness on my cheek, then let the breeze carry them away.

The old abandoned cabin that had been there since I was young was in further disrepair, a loose padlock on the door's latch. I curiously opened it to expose the one-room interior with a woodstove. Cocoa walked in and sniffed a saucepan on top of a bucket. I felt sick to my stomach when I realized what this building was being used for.

The boarded-up windows had distinctive gaps precisely big enough for the head of a rifle to fit through. I had to get out of there. I contemplated returning with a hammer and dismantling the boards so at least the animals could catch the scent of the hunters inside and be warned. The lock was too corroded to close, so I left the door wide open in protest. Maybe a skunk would spray inside and deter anyone from coming back.

We ventured through the field, passing the crab apple trees, and I picked up a fallen fruit and threw it to Cocoa. The earthy smell of plant matter filled the air as we went by the ancient hollowed-out tree near the deer beds. I looked at my companion who shared this sacred retreat with me. I caught myself thinking, wondering how I could contain this peace we had together and amidst nature. If only I could find a way to bring it with me everywhere I went, it would be a continually calming reality. Sadness crept in of leaving this serenity, the company I kept, this place I loved so much.

Here I was engaged and about to move across the world to marry the man I adored, but I started to fear losing Cocoa and the way the woods made me feel. It was like I was mourning a part of myself, that the weight of being an adult would prevent me from feeling this freedom again. I would be stuck in the monotony and predictability of the western world, becoming complacent to life and losing touch with the enchantment here.

The thought, the *push* that I had to strive for the "more" that everyone else seemed to be after nagged my mind and I felt inadequate. How could I be happy if I was inauthentic to the very grain of my being? My kind of more was different from what mainstream society could deliver. Maybe I was capable of attaining this elusive thing. Maybe I already knew the answer...

A loud huffing sound tore me from my pondering. Cocoa and I froze in our tracks, facing the direction of the noise. It became raspy. We looked at each other, her nose slanted into the air, and I could tell she was alarmed as her hairs stood up. We waited, unmoving. I could feel my heart pounding, its volume made me afraid I would give away our location, but the wind was blowing in our favor. Still, I couldn't deny the senses of the wild.

Standing strong, I clapped in loud, spaced-out succession. The sound stopped. Something in the woods beyond the rock wall and past the field trudged away, and we lingered until it was completely gone. Again, eyes had been on us, but none mine could see. Had it been a bear, a moose… Big Foot? Cocoa did a nervous half-jump toward me.

I patted her before walking to the rift in the road where the mountain spring flowed around the exposed rocks, eventually leading to the beaver pond next to a larger field. I brushed aside my alarm from the mysterious sound. Instinctively, I knew we were safe. Cocoa was confident again and climbed down to immerse herself in the water, swimming in a tight circle as she happily blew bubbles.

I found a spot to sit, looking at the hill ahead, recalling the time I convinced Katie to go off-roading in her "Barbie" jeep. I hadn't realized how steep and rocky it was, and there was no turning back. I directed her over this break in the road, and when she floored the engine, the vehicle came within a foot of hitting me as it surged across. Yet again, I had been protected by something more powerful than me.

I picked up a leaf and studied the veins, tearing to the main stem and tying it in a bow, then collected others to braid. I felt at peace, my mind at ease, truly nurtured by the natural wonders. Cocoa jumped onto the embankment, shook, and walked to me, swinging her bum against my arm to further dry herself.

"Oh, Cokie, you're such a funny bunny," I crooned to her. Eager to head home, we ran to the top of the driveway where she paused to grab another big stick. My body was energized as I raced her through the back paths. Rounding the corner into the yard, I was out of breath and collapsed into the hammock, my shoes covered with tree sap and pine needles. Cocoa dropped the stick and finally settled on the ground by my side.

I envisioned getting married at Leona's Beach, in the familiar setting of Elbow Pond and Ragged Mountain. I planned it with Mama as Cocoa scoped out the pond one afternoon. Paw would be brought in from the side path, his wheelchair rigged onto a trailer attached to a four-wheeler. I would walk down the steeper path that I had taken so often, this time to join Matt in the rock circle where we would exchange our vows.

I played it over and over in my head. It was going to be a small gathering with my family, Matt's parents, a couple of friends, and of course, Cocoa. It would be in October, presumably during the peak foliage. But then I started getting overwhelmed by the details of the reception. I wanted simplicity, yet it was somehow getting complicated, and the cost just seemed too exorbitant. I decided to put the planning on hold as I still hadn't heard from the Australian Government. Timing was everything.

I was working on the upstairs computer. Cocoa sat nearby, staring at me with a look of boredom. I couldn't take it and got up. As if she knew, she went to the far end of the piano, and I started our song. She sang out wholeheartedly, and I listened with rapture. Work could wait.

"Cokie, that's so pretty," I said, brimming with love. A catchy tune played faintly in the background. I turned it up and sang loudly, lifting Cocoa's front paws to dance with her. I was so happy. She broke into her high-pitched bark, and I chased her around. "I'm gonna get you!" I toppled onto the floorboards as she lapped at my face.

Mama's jeep barreled into the driveway and Cocoa went to the door, her tail bud motioning her excitement. "Who's here?!" I let her out and could see her exaggerated bum wag as she approached Mama's outstretched arms. I went back to the piano and tried to play the song from the radio.

"You have mail!" Mama called as she walked up the stairs, followed by Cocoa. Her expression told me it wasn't just any old bill. She handed me a business envelope with an official stamp on it from the Australian Government. I took a seat on the couch, my heart beating out of my chest. Mama sat beside me while Cocoa lay in front of us, watching closely.

I opened the envelope and found the stapled documents, my eyes focusing on the cover letter. *VISA GRANT NOTIFICATION...* I scanned the words. *A decision was taken to grant the applicant this visa.* It was really happening. "Oh yay! I can't believe it! I'm going to marry Matt and live with him in Australia!"

"Congratulations, Amandy!" Mama said with a big smile. Cocoa got up and wanted to get involved in the celebration, licking our faces and wagging her tail bud. That exhilarating moment was so profound until all of a sudden, my heart sank and I felt sick.

"That means I'm leaving you," I realized, looking from Mama to Cocoa. The time spent in this uplifting environment was slipping from my grasp. Uncontrollable tears streamed down my cheeks. How could this be so bittersweet?

The wind blew my long hair against Cocoa's coat, the strands a blend of bronze as though they were from one entity. I hugged my knees to my chest. Cocoa sat perfectly upright, her paws crossed daintily, and I fell into her endless eyes, way down to her beautiful soul. We gazed out at the woods in silent observation. There was no beginning and no end as sounds encircled us in a harmonious embrace. My body was numb with relaxation, accepting of this last occasion we shared in nature before I would delve into my new life so far away.

As hard as it was leaving my human family, especially my mother who had become such a dear friend, I felt utter devastation leaving Cocoa. I didn't know how to explain this to her, how long it would be before I would see her again. I read somewhere that time isn't a concept for animals because they live completely in the moment. That being said, a day alone without someone you love and expect to be there would feel like forever — waiting and waiting with anticipation.

I was filled with sadness thinking about this, swallowing my guilt while I packed the essentials. My loyal companion lay slumped, her sorrowful eyes giving away what she already knew was ahead. I wished there was some way she could come with me, but I could never take her from her home in the woods with Mama. I would have to learn how to hold her close in my heart.

CHAPTER SEVEN:
Over the Rainbow

Back to Brisbane to begin anew. I got lost in the time of year as the seasons of the Northern Hemisphere were so ingrained in me, I could no longer use them as a point of reference. November now delivered spring. Everything was in bloom, and the trees happily displayed their grandeur.

The large poinciana boldly marked the front of our yard. With green fern-like branches full of bright red flowers, the color combination reminded me that Christmas was around the corner. Birds foraged amongst the crown, plucking tiny seeds and light green worms to carry to their young. The bottlebrush tree next door attracted many colorful species — rainbow lorikeets, cockatoos, and noisy miners whose feisty squabbles caused Holly to bark with irritation.

The massive jacarandas lined the streets, and at night appeared to be covered with snow as the gentle moonlight washed over their lilac blossoms. But the simple frangipani with creamy white petals and a yellow center was my favorite, and I often tucked one behind my ear in island fashion before gifting it to the giant fig in the middle of the fields. As the leaves fluttered in the breeze, the scents of mock orange, lilly pilly, and jasmine mixed into a sweet fragrance like that of the wild berries at home.

Spring also meant nesting, and with this came territorial warfare from above. Cyclists sped by us as we walked along the track, their helmets looking alien with zip ties sticking out, all in an effort to discourage the swooping birds. Despite their friendly musical symphonies, magpies could be fierce protectors, while plovers were even more threatening with their wing spurs, shrieking and plummeting toward anyone who got too close.

⸺

The balmy air invited us to Moreton Bay, the gateway to Tangalooma Island. Matt and I made this our special place. Only an hour's boat ride and we were there amongst the brilliant sandhills and teal water that enticed us to jump in. I felt like a mermaid swimming freely until the thought of sharks pushed me closer to the shore. We ran up the steep slopes, plunking down to try and catch our breath while the spectacular panoramic view seemed to take it away again. It was distant from the hustle and bustle of the city, where we could be together in utter appreciation of the experience.

⸺

Outdoor markets were everywhere, varying for all tastes and interests. Seasonal produce, plants, crafts, clothing, and holiday stalls offered entertainment day and night. Melodious songs from buskers and friendly laughter drifted to my ears as we walked into our favorite one. The aroma of locally roasted coffee and homemade chai tea tempted us. Dogs were welcomed, triumphant to share this weekly outing with their families while meeting others.

It was a nourishing scene for the body, mind, and soul. The weather was hot, but the shade under the enormous trees made it just cool enough to be tolerable. This was our weekly routine of buying fresh organic food, a myriad of colors offering holistic nutrition, almost all of it straight from the farmers who grew it. The pied piper played his melody, his mysteriously dark eyes drawing me in. I was a snake being charmed until children chasing one another brushed past, jolting me from the spell.

A man shouted his latest bargain, and the banana farmer's produce depleted quickly as I hurried to get my share. The lean, white-haired man with a shy demeanor greeted me. Onward to the "Happy Farmers" for their raw honey and array of Chinese herbs, then to get Adam's greens grown on Tamborine Mountain in mineral-rich soil. The soft-spoken guy wearing a large brimmed hat and baggy clothes sold me some raw macadamias and almonds.

I perused the organic cotton shirts, then skimmed my hand over the woven fibers of colorful Fairtrade baskets, valuing their stories and craftsmanship. The alternative cleaning products, Himalayan salt lamps, recycled stationery, bamboo clothing, vegan chocolate, handmade candles, sweet baked goods… There was always something new to distract me, and sometimes I stayed longer, my arms weighed down by the bulging hemp bags. One last stop in the city garden for some lavender and rosemary plants, then the drive home.

⇁

The initial challenge of driving on the left side of the road no longer posed a difficulty for me, but it was still surprising I didn't have to take a driver's test. My American license was instantly approved, somehow validating that I could faultlessly execute the differing road rules. I sat in the passenger seat for weeks before taking the wheel.

The spatial awareness was the hardest to compensate for when driving on the left side of the road, passing on the right, trying to reverse out of a long and narrow driveway while in the right-hand seat, "give way" to the opposite direction, and manually shift with my left hand. The same rules applied when walking in public spaces, on sidewalks, and even bike riding on a track. I finally transitioned with time and practice, and going back to American ways now took some getting used to.

At the airport, I had a couple minutes to call home. Mama picked up as the answering message started. "Good timing, Amandy—" She waited for the recording to play out. "We just got in from a walk. You'll get a kick out of this. Earlier, I was trying to finish the last chapter of a book and Cocoa came to my side, around the time we usually go on our afternoon walk. 'A few more pages and then we'll go,' I told her. I went back to reading but was distracted by the feeling of being watched.

"I glanced over to see her sitting up, completely still, looking straight at me without blinking once. She was so stern, like she was telepathically commanding me to move. I tried to continue reading, but her stare was too intense, so I gave in and closed the book. She jumped up victoriously and we were out the door!"

I laughed, imagining the scenario. Cocoa could be so stubborn and persuasive, it was hard not to give in to her. "Well, Mama, you have a live-in exercise coach, that's for sure," I said. "Give her kisses for me. We are going to board the plane now. I can't believe I am about to get married!"

It was exactly how I saw it in my dream. The mountainous green edge next to the dazzling cerulean ocean. This was Lord Howe Island, and as we sat in the tiny airplane beginning the descent, it looked like paradise. The perfect place to elope. Peaceful, remote, romantic, and with no technological distractions.

The shuttle bus picked us up from the single-building airport and crawled along the winding road to Capella Lodge. Matt and I had booked for a week's holiday, deciding to invest in the best accommodation for our combined wedding and honeymoon. The resort faced the island's tallest mountain, the rolling pastures where cattle grazed, and the open ocean.

We hopped onto bikes and coasted down the hill toward town, passing a small beach and grassy knoll on the left. A sign read "Lover's Bay." Just a short walk and there it was, completely unobstructed — the grass, the ocean, the mountain — the site for our ceremony!

With very few vehicles on the roads and the speed limit being twenty-five kilometers, it felt as if the whole island was in slow motion. The road curved, and we cycled adjacent to the pristine coastline and through pockets of forest before meeting with our marriage celebrant. She was colorful, eccentric, and most importantly, organized. "Okay, where would you like to get married?" she asked.

"We've decided on Lover's Bay," I said. She nodded in agreement.

"That's a marvelous spot. Here is all the information. Choose your wording, then give me a call to finalize. My partner will be there to sign your certificate as a witness." It was as easy as that. Matt and I looked at each other with relief.

We found Ned's Beach hidden away down a long road past the main street shops. As the afternoon sun lowered in the sky, the clouds glowed pink. A few people snorkeled, while others threw bread into the water as large fish schooled around them. Our focus went to the same thing. A signature fin rose to the surface of the water right behind a boy who was splashing about.

"Shark!" Matt yelled. The boy laughed back.

"I know! There are heaps!" I was puzzled by his carefree response.

That night, we went to the lounge room for "nibblies" and drinks with the other guests, then had a scrumptious dinner. Cauliflower soup started us off, every last spoonful delectable. Fresh kingfish was the main course caught by one of the locals, but not from Ned's Beach. No fishing was allowed there for good reason. Dessert was simple but decadent, a chocolate indulgence that finished the meal on a velvety note. Matt and I treasured all the fine details.

―

The island offered so much. We walked, hiked, biked, kayaked, snorkeled, and even swam at Ned's Beach since being assured the sharks were only small and uninterested in us. I was definitely getting more confident in the water. I looked through my goggles as Matt followed a parrotfish who seemed to pose for him, swimming to one side, then flipping around to display his bright colors.

A three-foot reef shark passed by, and I grabbed the underwater camera to record him. Matt got some bread, returning to the water to feed the kingfish. "One just bit me!" he protested after throwing a few morsels in. I watched the fish swarm, their fins sweeping against my legs as the water became agitated during this mad competition for food.

―

Everywhere we went, there was a new discovery. A late morning hike up to Goat House Cave was the first time we passed the far end of the resort. We walked over a stock grid and huge cattle turned their attention our way. Matt stopped to take photos of them, their sleek ebony coats calling to the lens.

Red gums and strangler figs lured us to the track, with crisp earth smells invigorating our senses. "Hold onto the cable," Matt said as he moved up the slope. The ascent became very steep, my arms sore from steadying my weight, but the effort was well worth it. An immense cavernous rock marked our destination, and the entire island extended far below us, the vast ocean reflecting the midday sun. We could even see the shadowy figure of Balls Pyramid, the world's tallest sea stack, where ocean creatures thrived.

White birds with long red tail feathers glided before us, almost coming into contact with each other, soaring higher and flipping back, then plunging downward and curving up again, all the while singing their song. How free they must feel! It was like an orchestrated dance put on specifically for our entertainment. After such a special experience, a warm rain fell upon us.

It was our wedding day. My long hair was curled into soft ringlets with pink frangipanis woven through them, my makeup was done, and my nails were painted. I put on my simple pink dress, handmade earrings and necklace, and iridescent heels, then looked in the mirror. "I'm getting married," I said to my smiling reflection. *My next adventure.*

The professional photographer we had found on the island met me at the pathway leading to Lover's Bay. I walked along the grass, my heart racing. Around the bend was a small gathering of guests from the lodge, and in the distance was Matt, standing tall and handsome. A Celtic medley was cued up as I continued toward him. The celebrant initiated the ceremony, then we turned to face each other to exchange our vows.

Everything else faded as I gazed into Matt's gentle eyes, and I could feel the love we shared. Van Morrison's voice sang out. We were lost in an embrace, and in the splendor of the moment, my eyes brimmed with tears. The music played on as we signed the marriage certificate. The sun's warmth and magnificent illumination of the bay emphasized what my heart was feeling — that love was expansive, forever... That it knew no end.

⁓

We viewed the wedding disc the following morning. The first photo was a little fuzzy. The second was the same. As we skipped through, they got progressively worse, out of focus, some overexposed with the flash, others too dark. There was maybe a handful worth keeping, but the rest were terrible.

Matt called the photographer, who was quick to meet with us. "Mate, we've looked through the photos and they're really bad," he said. The man was taken aback.

"What do you mean?"

"We can't even tell it's us in most of them, they're so blurry." The joyful gleam in his eyes dulled, and he lowered his head.

"So many people have loved my work," he murmured. "I've never failed at this before." I felt his disappointment.

"There just aren't any that we would show people. Come and have a look for yourself." Matt opened the photos.

"I mustn't have had the settings adjusted right." He shook his head in disbelief.

"We know it wasn't intentional. Mistakes happen!" I tried to reassure him. "I saw the guests from here taking pictures, so we'll probably have some." This seemed to lift his spirits.

Fortunately, a few people came to us with their photos. There were two close-ups as we said our vows, an aerial view of the setting, and one of us signing the marriage certificate. At least we had some from the actual event, but I knew it wasn't enough. "Our families, friends... Everyone is going to expect more," I said. "And especially since none of them were here." Matt nodded.

It became common knowledge of the mishap, and we found out one of the chefs at the resort had a professional camera and took surf photos. He was happy to help us recreate the event. The next day, I went to have my hair and makeup done again, then met Matt and the new photographer at Lover's Bay at the original time of our wedding. Thankfully, the afternoon was just as sunny and beautiful. It wasn't long before we saw the impressive quality of the retakes and could move forward.

After an interesting talk about the flora and fauna that existed on the island, there was one thing that particularly intrigued me. I had to investigate further. As the last light drained from the sky, we took a golf cart to the forest where bioluminescent mushrooms supposedly grew. It was like something out of *Alice in Wonderland*. We drove around in the pitch dark, hearing many foreign sounds amongst the trees yet unable to spot the glowing fungi anywhere. But it didn't mean they didn't exist.

With only a couple of days left on the island, there was still so much to see. The private boat charter that had been gifted to us was next. Gearing up in wetsuits, flippers, goggles, and snorkels, we headed onto a glass-bottom boat called *Coral Princess*. Multi-colored fish of all sizes were everywhere as we explored the reef. I watched through my goggles, the sea seemingly breathing with the fluctuations of the current. Not a thought about sharks crossed my mind. The aquatic life was mystifying, and as the sun's rays sifted through the surface of the water, everything sparkled. We returned to the boat happily exhausted.

Out of nowhere, a wave rolled toward us, picking up in volume and rapidly approaching the side of the boat. The skipper tried to turn its direction, but it was too late. The cumbersome vessel couldn't move fast enough. The powerful wave lifted us into the air, the side of the boat riding it as we clung on in suspended animation.

I was staring down at Matt and the sharp reef behind him. But just as quickly as the wave had come, it was gone, and the boat smacked heavily onto the water. I looked over at the skipper, his face ashen. "That was all part of the program," he said with a smirk. I believed him for a minute and laughed uneasily with Matt. Our first days of being married, and it was truly turning out to be an adventure.

CHAPTER EIGHT:

Fresh Eyes

Upon our return to suburbia, things settled into routine. Married life didn't seem to be anything extraordinary, but somehow I had that expectation. It was strange calling Matt my husband. Husband. How mature.

I looked forward to our weekend trips to visit Chris and Melina, who lived in a beautiful leafy town that reminded me of my own. Chris and Matt's bond was echoed in Melina and my friendship, as we shared many similarities. I could let go of all my insecurities and talk with her about everything. She became a rock for me — a recognized soul sister and confidante. Melina introduced me to chakra meditation, energy healing, and brought to my awareness my addiction to sugar. I needed all the help I could get as the challenges from my move overseas erupted.

I started feeling the boundaries of where I lived. The sun felt more intense, singeing, like I was trapped in an oven. I began to fear it as I saw people of all ages with mottled, victimized skin, oftentimes with bandages plastered on their faces and limbs. After all, the Sunshine State held the title as the skin cancer capital of the world. The fact lingered in the back of my mind as I noticed my own skin getting freckled and patchy with sunspots.

My "good" skin would only last so long if I wasn't careful. I had to be sun smart by wearing hats and timing my exposure, going out early in the morning or in the evening when the ultraviolet rays were the weakest. I slathered on sunscreen but then questioned its ingredients, wondering if they contributed to the development of melanomas. It frustrated me that I couldn't have the same freedom of being outside like where I grew up.

There were more ramifications due to the shift in hemisphere and climate. Within a year of living in Queensland, I developed allergies for the first time. I couldn't go anywhere without a box of tissues, my eyes squinty and red, my nose dripping profusely. Then a fungus began to grow on my skin. These light brown patches were scattered all over my body. I continuously washed with a tea tree solution and applied an antifungal cream to the spots until they finally disappeared without recurrence.

I swore when a green ant first bit me, it would be the last bite. The insect looked comparable to the harmless ones from home too, but I quickly learned to beware of them. I had never experienced something as painful. Then came the bindii — a dried weed that pricked the softest part of my sole, making it bleed, and stuck there obstinately until I pulled it out. It was obvious I could no longer take for granted being barefoot on the grass.

Cane toads and paralysis ticks were of concern as they could kill a dog, and I worried about Holly. She had a narrow escape from the poison of a cane toad years ago. Luckily, Matt saw the froth on her tongue and washed it out before she ingested it. The ticks were easier to ward off with a preventative tablet, but it wasn't completely fool-proof. I repeatedly checked her, especially in the warmer months.

Having neighbors living so close by weighed on me. It was like someone was always watching when I stepped outside, different from being watched by the hidden creatures back home. I craved the expanse and seclusion the woods offered. Inside the fencing of six-hundred square meters, it was as if I was a caged animal, unable to run wild and free. Various sounds in the neighborhood were persistently there — the hum of a lawn mower, an argument, kitchen clatter, televisions blaring... I yearned for privacy.

I missed my family and those once underappreciated occasions. My siblings settled down and began their own families. I craved being a part of their lives, for their children to know me. I was suddenly at a standstill, while everyone else had moved on. The biggest gaping hole was from missing Cocoa. How strongly I felt the distance from her. When would I see her next?

For as many new memories as I made, I remained stuck. I realized that my heart was in two places, and I was in limbo. I had started over in another country, but I couldn't let go of home. Home was still in the woods, running on the pine needle paths with Cocoa, taking in the seasonal changes of New England. I was lost in time as it was Christmas again, but in Brisbane, it was like the summers of my childhood. I actually craved the cold, relief from the rising heat and humidity of Queensland. Most of all, I wanted to escape from this grown up life I struggled to live as I was clouded with its limitations.

This mental and emotional reluctance to accept where I was physically came at a cost, and it wasn't only affecting me, it was affecting my marriage. I went from job to job, unmotivated, unhappy, not taking responsibility for my choices. My outlook of adventure and living in the moment had changed as I stopped doing that, eagerly counting the days before my next visit home.

Was it the pull of the grass being greener elsewhere? The "what if?" Would I constantly be after the elusive? I was solely seeing the shortcomings of my commitment, and having no inclination of anything concrete for my future now seemed liberating.

I began to resent all that I was so ready to take up in this whirlwind of a romance, in this whirlwind of a decision. And the resentment turned bitter. I was spiraling downward as negative thoughts enveloped me. I was envious of Matt living close to his family, for not having to sacrifice anything, for getting the best of both worlds. I recalled my conversation with him about moving to Australia. I was so confident it would all work out smoothly, that the distance wouldn't prove a challenge. How could it? I had fallen in love, wasn't that enough? Had my belief in fairytales skewed reality?

The transition proved drastic and kinks unraveled. The longer I lived away, the harder it got. I continually compared the two places, favoring what I had known for the longest, and my eyes began to glaze over as I was losing sight of the ever-present beauty that surrounded me.

―

I watched Holly gracefully run across the field. My body felt sedentary and devoid of natural drive. I pushed myself to chase her before pausing in front of the shaded gum trees, haunting with their blue-gray color. Holly crouched into a bowing position, her eyes glued to the frisbee on the grass near me. Her ears stood up, alert, and she was poised with precision.

I could tell she was tired, but her pedigree instinct prevailed. "One more throw, Hol," I said. I had to stop her. So integral to her nature was her unwillingness to quit. Her push, her endurance. I realized that this was somehow helping me drive through the pain I was feeling from the distance, change, and regret. She was drawing me away from a pessimistic outlook, pulling me out of the pit of despair I was succumbing to. She was reminding me to choose the present moment.

I called Mama shortly after having my breakfast. She was just finishing her day, relaxing with a cup of tea. I pined for that shared company, playing Scrabble together while Cocoa rested under the table, warming my feet. At least we could keep up our discussions. She listened as I told her about my latest health studies.

"Amandy, can you hold on a minute?" she asked. "Cocoa's being very quiet and I think she's up to something." I giggled and waited. I knew Cocoa didn't like the phone, computer, or when Mama was reading and she wanted to go for a walk. She had an abundance of energy and showed her irritation when she couldn't expend it. Yet even when she was outside alone, her loyal and protective nature dominated as she never wandered far despite the acres of woods that tempted her.

"Cocoa!" I heard Mama grumble before returning to the phone. "She's chewed holes in my new fleece blanket. We didn't go out for a walk because it was raining all day. She's upset and wants my attention." I couldn't help but laugh. "It's the third blanket she's done that to," she complained.

"Well, she's definitely telling you something," I said.

"I know… I'd better go and play piano for her. That might change her mood."

"Can I listen?"

"Sure, I'll just bring the phone up. C'mon, Cokie, want to sing?" I heard Mama walk up the stairs and set the phone down. She dabbled on the keys. Chopsticks, "Mama-style." Cocoa let out a few high-pitched, drawn-out whimpers before breaking into her full-bellied laments. It was music to my ears. I could see myself sitting on the worn floorboards by the red woodstove, watching as the duo performed.

—

Moving along the ocean boardwalk with Holly, I was lost in my thoughts again, feeling homesick. A man resembling a tropical Santa Claus nodded at me as we walked opposite ways. "G'day," he said, "beautiful dog you have."

"Thank you. This is Holly." She stopped to sniff his outstretched hand and wagged her tail. He was cleared. "How are you?"

"I'm having a good morning. How're you going?"

"Fine, thanks. It's so calming here." I found myself glossing over my sadness, but he seemed unconvinced.

"Mind if I walk with you a little?"

"Sure. We're just going up to the beach," I said. He nodded.

"So, where's that accent from?"

"The States. But a lot of people say I sound Canadian, even my husband said that when we first met. I don't know if I'll ever lose it. I talk to my family almost every day, so they keep my ear trained."

"Family," he said. "I've been married twice. My first wife was my greatest love, and I had two wonderful children with her. But then I got silly and lost everyone. It's funny where life takes you. I was the happiest with her." His gaze was set on the water in a moment of reflection. "My second wife, well, she's a bit colorful," he chuckled. "So, are you happy in your marriage?" I was surprised by this personal question from a stranger and hesitated before responding.

"Well, I am married to an honest man I love…"

"Is he good to you?"

"Yes. He's so thoughtful and caring. I suppose I've been stirring up our relationship, though. I'm just having a hard time living so far away from home," I confessed. "My heart is torn between two places." Why was it so easy to say this to a complete stranger? I don't think I had ever admitted this out loud. It was oddly cathartic.

There was a break in the conversation before the man replied. "The way I see it is that you have an abundance of happiness wherever you are. When you're here, you're with your beloved husband in this great country. And when you're over there visiting your family, you can savor that time. You're never at a loss because you always have love with you. It's a win-win situation."

His insight was compelling. "Thank you, that really helps…" Holly stopped near the pier and looked toward the beach.

"You don't have to give up anything." He was adamant.

"I appreciate your wisdom," I said, thanking him again.

"Enjoy your day." He smiled and turned back down the boardwalk. I let out a sigh. As I have heard, people come into your life for a reason, a season, or a lifetime. This stranger certainly gave me an enlightening perspective to consider.

I woke up from a nightmare where Mama died and Cocoa was alone in the woods. I called home right away and was comforted upon hearing my mother's voice. I recounted the horrible dream. "Well, don't worry, I'm still breathing!" she said. "Wait until you hear the latest with Cocoa." My heart pounded.

"She's okay?" I felt a lump form in my throat.

"She's fine. A few days ago, I let her outside and did some chores around the house. I happened to glance out and saw her lying by the woodshed. I opened the door and she briefly acknowledged me but stayed put and stared down at her paws. 'What do you have?' I asked her. She looked at me, then at her paws again. I could see something wiggling while she just waited there, holding it protectively. It was a baby bird who must have fallen from her nest!"

"Oh wow! And Cocoa was consoling her!" I imagined the scene of "Guardian Cocoa," cradling the little being in her big paws.

"Then I asked her, 'Can I help?' and she gazed at me with those intense eyes of hers, so concerned as I reached down to take the tweeting bird. Her ears perked up in response. 'Don't worry,' I told her, 'I'll put her safely here,' and I hid her under some leaves in the flower pot on the picnic table. Cocoa walked over to investigate, and as if satisfied, she came back inside with me. The next day, the chick was gone."

"Oh, she doesn't cease to amaze me," I said. "Thanks for sharing that story, Mama! I feel better already. I'm so glad you two are together in the woods." I hung up with no more thought of my nightmare.

Mama was coming to Australia to make her long-ago wish come true. She arrived in early June, missing the heat and humidity of summer. I was used to being the one taking the big trips, so it was exciting to have someone visit me. When she walked into the airport lobby, I cheered and ran to her.

"Welcome, Brendy, how was the trip?" Matt gave her a big hug and grabbed her luggage.

"It's good to be here! I had three seats to myself, so it was pretty comfortable."

"That's the best, especially for all those hours. We have everything set up for you at home. Some delicious brekkie, tea…" I rambled on, staring at my mother in astonishment that she was really in front of me. "Was Cokie upset to see you leave?"

"She looked at my bags suspiciously at first, but because she was going on the ride to Katie's, she seemed okay. I'm just glad that she's staying with her," Mama said.

"Me too," I agreed. "Holly is going to be so excited to have you stay."

And boy was she ever! Mama entertained her ball-focused drive right away and gave her ample attention. We shared a tropical breakfast on the veranda facing the splendid poinciana tree, listening to her talk about her travels through Europe, the plentiful adventures she had, the free spirit she was.

I remembered telling her stories like they were my own. I wished I could time-travel to live them with her — to ski every day in the Swiss Alps while working at a bed and breakfast, to see the leprechaun who jumped in the window on that foggy night in Ireland, to experience the haunting nature of the Loch Ness… Now, in a different way, I was getting my wish.

There was so much ahead of us. I had planned a full two weeks, having learned from Katie's visit to include some downtime too. Mama was still as outgoing as I pictured her to be, after all, she had just taken the longest trip of her life. She was up for anything.

On the drive to meet Chris and Melina, Mama stared out at the scenery. "Some of these areas remind me of home," she said as we neared their place. I agreed. Our friends proved to be as hospitable as ever, and conversation was easy with much laughter around a campfire. The Southern Cross shone brightly in the starry sky as the green tree frogs chorused on.

The Big Pineapple markets were the next morning. Mama was astounded by all the fresh food, the sweetest pineapples she had ever tasted, and the energetically vibrant atmosphere. We observed a living statue, her skin painted silver, and took a photo before throwing a gold coin into her collection hat. Mama understood that the one and two dollar coins quickly added up, and the colorful play-like notes were durable, washable, and of definite value.

Going to the world-famous Australia Zoo was an essential part of the itinerary to see all the native fauna. At the entrance, Mama was greeted by a special owl visiting the grounds. We sat in the stands to watch various animals, completely awed by the huge saltwater crocodile who burst out of the water to catch food dropped by a trainer.

When I first visited in 2006, I had been in the same stands during a performance by Bindi Irwin and glanced over to see Steve and the rest of the family. I was a bit star-struck. Steve Irwin was my initial draw to Australia ever since I started watching *The Crocodile Hunter* my last year in college. His enthusiastic introduction to the different animals and their environments intrigued me so much, I decided to travel to the vast country.

―

We hosted a "barbie" that weekend, attended by family and friends. I watched Mama conversing, smiling frequently, nodding, and laughing as she tried to interpret the accents and jargon. I was immensely proud to introduce my mother and stand beside her as her daughter.

On a walk later, we stopped to visit the horses in the rehoming lot nearby. Sunlight cascaded off their strong bodies as they moved toward Mama. She gently spoke to them. Holly gave us her signal to move on, and we continued along the creek and through the fields where she happily ran after her ball. We lingered at the giant fig trees. Everything was thriving and green, a far cry from the former drought conditions.

"I rarely see snakes," I said. "They're supposedly in the bushes." I had seen two snakes in my hundreds of walks with Holly, but I was still cautious. "The first one, a red-bellied black, was only a foot away from where she was sniffing the ground, but she didn't take notice. I slowly clipped the leash onto her harness and moved back. Luckily, the snake wasn't bothered and slithered under some leaves." Mama sighed with relief.

"You really have a lot here — nice paths to walk with Holly, a good support network of people, interesting things all around. It's wonderful."

"I just really miss home and our family. I can't let go of the freedom I feel there, of the woods, my adventures with Cokie..." I trailed off. Mama understood.

"You don't have to let go of home. You will always have a place there and can return to that sense of freedom anytime." She wrapped her arm around my shoulder. "You remain in our hearts despite the distance." I took a deep breath in contemplation, the breeze seemingly conducting my emotion. I was trying to see my new home through fresh eyes as my mother offered her perceptions.

We ran from the train to pick up the river cruise to Lone Pine Koala Sanctuary. It was cold along the brown water, and we kept changing seats to be in the warmth of the winter sun. The boat passed by Brisbane City, then the surroundings became more scenic with nature. A water dragon sitting on the jetty welcomed us to the leafy environment of Fig Tree Pocket.

My mother seemed to charm the animal kingdom. I recalled her innate ease with all the creatures who readily approached her, and today was no different. She had grain in her hand, as the other visitors did, yet she was the one to have drawn a crowd. Three large kangaroos and several ducks were simultaneously eating from her palm. She started laughing at a kookaburra, and right away, he laughed back. Even the koala she was holding wanted to get closer to her. She was a wildlife magnet. There was just *something* about Mama.

After the long isolated road to Rainbow Beach, we arrived at the same villa Matt had taken me to a couple years ago. I motioned for Mama to follow me outside and led her down a tunnel-like path that brought us to a beach. "Voila!" I did pirouettes, stretching my limbs as I raced across the sand, turning to see Mama test the water, foamy with bubbles. In the late afternoon light, we wrote in the sand, "Mama in Australia, 2012."

We met our tour group on the barge to Fraser Island at dawn. It was chilly as the wind picked up, the trees blocking out the sun's emerging position. Waiting on land was our guide — a man who very much resembled the iconic "Crocodile Dundee." We loaded into a bus, and it jolted about as he skillfully swerved from the rising tide.

The beach widened, the ride becoming smoother. We chatted with some of the people in the group, including a Swiss guy on vacation. Mama told him of when she worked in Switzerland, and his eyes lit up. "Ah, yes, the Hotel Bolgenschanze, I know of it! I've been there!" Mama smiled excitedly, and the two were lost in conversation.

The beaches, perched lakes, dunes, rainforest, creeks, shipwreck… I was as amazed as Mama, even on my third visit. We hiked up to Indian Head. Some girls were taking close-up pictures of a snake basking in the sun, and later found out it was a coastal taipan, one of the most highly venomous species.

"Katie and I went swimming there," I said, pointing at the pristine beach in the near distance. Mr. Dundee overheard.

"That's a shark breeding ground," he warned. I felt a rush of adrenaline, learning that our previous tour guide had been fired for many reasons. At last we reached the Champagne Pools, a site I had never experienced due to the high tides. It lived up to its name as water crashed and frothed into the natural rock spa formations in a climax of natural wonder.

The scenes sparked creative interpretation. A hill with miniature piles of crusted earth looked like a model of a Greek city, while the dips in the sandy landscape blocked out view of the ocean and we were in the Sahara. Mama posed with the local newspaper before we glided down the dunes to the emerald green Lake Wabi, gleaming in the sun.

Back on the beach, we drove by a washed-up whale carcass. A dingo fed on it as others joined in. We were truly witnessing the circle of life. A few kilometers along, the bus suddenly halted to a stop, the tires spinning into the soft sand. It was bogged. We got out and helped the tour guide shovel around the wheels until a land cruiser pulled up and four shirtless guys jumped out, clad in aviator sunglasses and flirty smiles. As soon as we heard their accents, Mama and I started giggling. "Well, you've definitely had a dose of Switzerland!" I whispered through a smirk.

On our final evening there, we trekked out of the resort to watch the surf at its record height from the recent king tide. The sky blushed peach. Just as it had been for Katie and me, Mama's favorite excursion was Fraser Island. It was a wondrous place, a destined adventure.

Noosa was where I first fell in love with Australia. The most beautiful part of this seaside town lay in the national park there.

I had been through it more times than I could remember, yet there was always something new and exciting along the coastal and inland tracks.

As we walked toward the information center, the dreary sky loomed overhead. The spikey volume of the pandanus framed the foreground, and storm clouds accumulated out at sea. Surfers looked like vulnerable black seals bobbing in the water as they waited for the perfect wave. A few ventured closer to the jagged outcrop of rocks, slippery with ocean spray.

Matt spotted a pod of dolphins that quickly disappeared into the choppy water. The smell of eucalyptus was everywhere, and we combed the bushy tree-line for koalas. None in sight. Continuing in and out of tall forests and shrubby vegetation, we arrived at the best location for coastal views. I turned to Mama.

"Thank you for being here."

"I'm so happy to be! To see this beautiful land, the wildlife, to spend time with you and Matt, meet his family and friends… It's all been so wonderful," she said, smiling at the open ocean. I indicated to the sand strip in the distance.

"That's a nudist beach." I grinned. Talk about ultimate freedom.

We were lost in the peaceful clatter of nature's songs amidst the inland track. The path wove through diverse vegetation and into a forest with short trees with green, afro-like needles weeping outward. We paused to study the fascinating swirls left behind from moths in the towering scribbly gums' bark. Streams trickled along rock beds, fallen branches mimicked snakes waiting to strike our tender ankles, and strange insects went about their own missions. The day seemed to smile at us as it became sunny at the end of the walk.

Matt, Mama, and I flew to Sydney to sightsee, but unbeknownst to my mother, we had something extra special planned. Our night began with a fancy dinner in full view of Sydney Harbour. Looking gorgeous in her cocktail dress, Mama was modest and graceful as she ate the rich cuisine, almost humbled, making me uncomfortable with my nonchalant attitude about it. I didn't like that I was taking it for granted and quickly tried to dismiss this part of myself.

"Well, Mama, after this we are going to see a dance performance at the Sydney Opera House!" I revealed the surprise.

"Wow!" Mama was awestruck. We walked to the iconic place, and I felt my own excitement intensify as we took our seats. The lighting was dim, casting shadows around the daring angles of the space. The music started and the intrigue built with the varied movement, bright colors, sounds, and storyline, creating a spectacular experience. It was the rhythm of emotions, a performance of existence.

I watched Mama say goodbye to Holly, and my mind drifted to my goodbyes with Cocoa. The unrestrained tears, the heart-wrenching moment of the final parting. But the reunions brought such wonderful sweetness, and Mama would get that before long. At the airport again, it seemed like life was on fast forward. "Thank you for the adventure," I said, thinking of all the stories we could now share. She smiled warmly as she scrunched her fingers into her wave.

The plane taxied to the runway and was soon skyward. I waved frantically as if she could see me from her tiny window, then wiped my tears when Matt hugged me close. Holly happily greeted us upon our return. As I crouched down to pat her, I noticed that her honey brown eyes were reminiscent of Mama's, both in color and energy, beacons of unconditional love. What a glorious discovery.

───

It started raining from a partly sunny sky. I felt light-footed with anticipation as I ran outside to find a rainbow. A V-formation of ibises, their wings swishing in synchronized movement, flew overhead. And there it was in full view, the rainbow stretching the extent of the skyline. I smiled. Ever since I was little, I would search for them, imagining myself sliding across the brilliant colors to a fantastical world. Mama's words rang in my ears, "*Rainbows are a sign of peace and hope. Of God's blessing.*"

I had never seen so many rainbows until living in Australia, where there were quite often double ones. As a girl struggling to be an adult, I clung onto the feeling they brought me for more hope. For more meaning. That wonderment they evoke was a little piece of childlike magic.

CHAPTER NINE:

Home

I could hear Cocoa at the top of the staircase and strained to see her figure in the shadows, hesitantly standing there, seemingly bigger than I remembered her. "Cokie! It's just me!" I called out. She whimpered with utter delight and rushed down the stairs toward me, struggling to walk across the floor. Her back end and tail bud wagged with uncontrollable enthusiasm while a little stream of pee confirmed her elation.

Her cries were prolonged and unlike any other greeting, as if she was singing our sorrows from being parted for so long, as if she knew the rollercoaster of difficulties I had faced in being away. She fell onto my lap, into my open arms, and I held her tight as I sobbed with happiness. She showered my face with kisses, and along with her verbalizations, the two of us were a chorus of reuniting friendship. If I could capture that emotion in a bottle, it would be pure joy. Unspoiled, untainted, authentic joy. "I missed you so much," I cried, my heart bursting with love.

I gazed into her familiar eyes, not sure how she was going to react to the next surprise. "Cokie, someone else is here too…" She bolted out the door.

"Cocoa!" Matt smiled broadly. Slowly curling into her worm-like position while her tail bud moved vigorously, she entangled herself in his welcoming arms, her eyes undeniably loving when she looked up and licked his cheek. Tears wet my face as I watched this incredible reception so entirely different from the first one — the exact connection I was hoping for now shared.

Matt and I had returned as newlyweds. Despite the lengthy travel, it was astonishing to think that across the world was only a day away. No matter how challenging it was to be separated from so much I loved, I had to be thankful for that. And now my husband would see further into the vibrant world my home was, in a season he was yet to experience.

The scenery was lush and green, and the foliage hadn't started changing aside from the deep red of the swamp maples. The woods were filled with noise. It was the best weather to traverse the countryside in the cool air and without bugs. We shared most of our adventures this time and it was different, even more expansive.

I observed Cocoa's increasing love for Matt to the point where he was her only focus, and I couldn't have been happier. He was finally seeing her capability for the ceaseless adoration that had so marked my heart. It was like he was let in on a secret as he caught a glimpse of the enchanting environment in the company we held. I was watching the synchronicity of my worlds aligning with Cocoa's acceptance of the man I married.

It was a calm winter morning, and a fresh blanket of snow covered the ground. Cocoa stared at me intently, nosing toward the door. As I held it open for her to venture out, I scooped some snow off the solar lamp, formed a snowball, and threw it, immediately catching her attention. My inner child poked at me.

Cocoa turned, a sprinkling of snow dotted her nose and continued to the top of her head. She bent down for another mouthful. "I'll be right back!" I shut the door and ran upstairs to get into warm clothes. "Wanna come out?" I asked Matt as I put on a heavy vest. He looked so cozy in his flannels that his answer was predictable.

Cocoa was eagerly waiting outside. I plunged into the snow, moving my arms and legs to make an angel before being pounced on by my energetic pup. She broke into a super-speed run around me. The cold nipped at my nose, but it felt good, and I began rolling the base of a snowman. Cocoa barked hysterically as she bounded at the formation. I tossed a snowball to divert her attention, and she jumped up to catch it, the melting ice seeping from the corners of her mouth as she ogled my attempted snowman.

In between heaving snowballs to distract her, I managed to finish the bottom. Just when I rolled it to my desired spot in the yard, Cocoa leapt up and took a bite out of the side. "Cokie!" I laughed at her feistiness. "Oh well, that's easy to fix." I scooped up more snow, pressing it in to fill the void. Ready to make the next ball, it was as if she read my thoughts and was at me, forbidding my progression. I sped up and completed it, albeit with a few nips at my mittens, my ears ringing from her vocal antics. I put the midsection on the base.

Cocoa paused when Mama joined us, coming to my aid by throwing some snowballs toward the cabin. I took advantage of the brief intervention and shuffled to get the head on the body. *Phew!* Cocoa looked at me, seemingly squinting with disapproval. She didn't like this large white being I had constructed, and I wasn't finished. "Very good, Amandy," Mama said, "how about some features?"

Now I had charcoal from the stove ash to make eyes, a carrot for the nose, and raisins to form the mouth. "Can you spare three acorns from Cocoa's stash? They'd make cute buttons," I said. Mama closed the door briefly before delivering my request. Cocoa sat sulking as she watched me carefully dig holes to hold the features and stick kindling into the sides as arms. Almost there. I felt her skeptical stare. "Just a few more things, Cokie." I ran up the outside staircase and indoors to get some mittens knitted by my grandmother, a wool hat, and scarf.

When I returned to the snowman, two of the acorn buttons had fallen. "I mustn't have put them in deep enough," I said to Cocoa, who was sitting in the same place I left her. I dug the holes deeper and replaced them, adding some sticky snow as a seal. I put the mittens on the kindling arms, set the hat on the head, and wrapped the scarf around the neck.

I marveled at my creation. "Pretty cool, huh, girl?" Cocoa looked at me, then at the snowman, staring him down, very clearly not liking his existence. I couldn't help but feel excited as this was the first snowman I had made since my childhood. "Mama, Matt, come outside!" I knocked on the glass of the front door. When I rejoined Mr. Snowman, his smile wasn't the same. A few raisins had completely vanished. Cocoa sat like a statue, perhaps a little closer to him than before. *As with the acorns, I mustn't have secured the raisins enough,* I thought.

I ran to the door again, and Mama replenished my supply. "One minute until the unveiling," I said, hustling to my project, stopping in my tracks as the incomplete face peered at me strangely. A half-eaten carrot lay on the ground. Now I knew the culprit. She was still, with somewhat of a smug demeanor. "Cocoa, did you do this to my snowman?" I scolded. She seemed to roll her eyes at me. I picked up the carrot stub and tossed it. Mama giggled.

"I'll get another one," she said. Cocoa moved out of view. In the momentary stillness, I stopped to survey the yard. Beautiful, peaceful white snow. I had a renewed love for it. The door opened and Mama handed me a carrot for Cocoa's nemesis.

This time, there was something seriously wrong. A kindling arm and a mitten hand were missing. Cocoa was nearby, watching me attentively. I couldn't help but crack up — she was a little magician. Just when I noticed the kindling and mitten half under her, she picked up the mitten and took off. I ran up the driveway after her, then doubled back.

"Quick! I have to fix this snowman and take a picture before she totally dismembers him!" I yelled. Matt was assessing the scene with a grin. I pulled a reluctant Cocoa close, and Mama snapped a shot of us. "Okay, girl," I said. Our eyes met. "I'm going inside for some hot chocolate. How about a treat?" She made no move to go with me and I conceded. The snowman was hers.

That afternoon, I went out to see what damage had been done by the visibly guilty offender. Mr. Snowman no longer had a recognizable face. Only smeared stains remained of the charcoal eyes, the acorn buttons had been chomped on and discarded, the raisin mouth was gone, and there were little remnants of carrot on the ground. His scarf was intact, but his hat had fallen, one arm was half broken, and both mittens had disappeared. It was a sorry sight.

"Cocoa!" She grabbed the hat and bolted as I chased her across the yard and back to the dismantled snowman. She took an enormous bite out of him before settling onto the snowbank with me. I chuckled. "You're such a brat." She responded with a big lap to my cheek. With her, everything was so much fun. I felt refreshed and lighthearted and couldn't help but think she had staged the entire charade for that outcome. We sat quietly as the white setting was dimmed by dusk.

I am photographing Cocoa with Matt's professional camera. She doesn't care for it and turns away, perched upon the top landing of the outside staircase. Her paws dangle lazily over the platform, and she methodically scans the front yard, perking her ears slightly to something soundless to mine.

Her face has matured, that puppy chubbiness long gone, replaced with lean, sculpted cheekbones. Her eyebrows are pulled together in concentration. A part forms above her eyes, in the middle of her forehead, and gently dissipates upward. Her ears are surrounded by wispy offshoots of fine auburn hair while blond feather-like strands crimp to form smooth, nested pockets behind them, reminding me of silky milkweed. I pause to brush my fingers through their softness before sneaking in more shots.

Her eraser nose now bears marks undoubtedly from her wild adventures in the woods. The sides of her mouth sag, then contour up to reveal a curled lip with tiny bumps. The little white tuft remains at the tip of her chin and raises to meet her pursed, solemn expression. She holds her body proudly, showing its length as she stretches her back legs, reclining her midsection like a dozing lioness.

She glances at the lens disapprovingly and I capture her distant gaze, locked in a meditative trance. She is stunning, majestic, a being from another world. I am flooded with a newfound love for her, breathless in appreciation for who she is. She continues to surprise and amaze me the more time goes by. The more she ages, the more she blossoms, and I am lucky to be a witness to her profound depth.

Barb had started a farm. "Cocoa, lead the way!" Mama said as we headed there one day. From a distance, camel-like creatures grazed with what seemed to be some very woolly-looking sheep. Cocoa barreled down the hill and the sheep dispersed, but the others just watched, clearly intrigued. She slowed her advance, cautiously walking to their fenced boundary.

"This is Winston," Mama introduced us. "He's a llama and will alert everyone of any danger." She indicated to the impressive, over six-foot tall animal with a black tail that stood out against his predominantly white coat. His eyelashes resembled white feathers waving as he blinked, bringing attention to his big brown eyes. He bent his long neck toward Cocoa, who lowered her head and peeked at him bashfully.

"Meet Reginald and Vinnie, the alpacas." Mama pointed to the auburn creatures, two additional sets of big eyes peering around Winston. Meanwhile, the shaggy sheep stepped closer. "These girls are Lavender and Mahalia. They look like sheep, but they're actually Angora goats. Barb plans on making sweaters from their wool." It was hard to see their faces under the guise of their thick coats, but at the right angle, I noticed their striking ice-blue eyes.

All the animals observed Cocoa as if trying to figure her out. They moved in even closer. Apparently, she didn't pose a threat as she shyly investigated her onlookers, almost touching noses with Winston as he put his face near hers. From where I stood, Cocoa appeared to be a combination of the alpacas' color, with the voluminous coat of the goats. Three more family members showed themselves. "That's Clover, Licorice, and Mocha." Mama beckoned to the male goats who were mostly interested in nibbling at our sleeves. Licorice backed up timidly to hide inside the shed.

There was barking behind us, and we could see Suka's face in the upstairs window. "I'll let him out," Mama said. Cocoa was exploring the mounds of hay when he came charging down the hill, headed for the animals. They frantically scattered as he approached the fence with his fiercest expression. Seemingly content with this display of dominance, he greeted Cocoa.

"Come on, guys, I have biscuits." Mama tried to lure them away from the droppings they were feasting on. Winston and the alpacas bravely crept closer, gaping at Cocoa until Suka spooked them again. "Well, you've met all the inhabitants of Winter Tales Farm," my mother happily announced.

Many eyes watched our retreat. Suka and Cocoa raced through the field, and we continued along the path to the pond. It was cool, and the plentiful pine needles made our steps inaudible. Suka disappeared into the forest to do his usual roaming while Cocoa remained a few paces ahead of us, turning back frequently to ensure her pack was following.

I rummaged through my dresser drawers and found the green, plaid flannel shirt I was searching for. It had once been my father's but no longer fit him, so I happily took it over. It smelled of wood smoke and patchouli. I threw on some jeans, thick socks on my icy feet, and a hat and scarf, making my way downstairs to put on boots and sort through the leather gloves before joining my eager co-worker outside.

She yipped with excitement as I grabbed an acorn and tossed it past her. Posed in her goalie stance, she waited. The game carried on. I picked up a handful and she charged at me. "Back it up, Cokie," I said in a deep voice, motioning to her. She shimmied backward, and I threw the rest of them. "Okay, girl, let's go to the paths!" I took a box from the shed and headed to my favorite spot to find kindling.

There was a definite chill in the air, but it was deeply refreshing as it filled my lungs. I loved being out there cleaning the paths of debris. I was quick to judge the branches, which ones were dry and burnable to keep, and those that were wet or pine to leave. I picked up a long piece, its bark peeling, and stomped my foot in the middle to break it. This wasn't a chore to me, it was more like therapy — a session with nature and Cocoa. She scoped out the surroundings, alert with concentration until she ran toward me with an oversized branch in her mouth and another chase began.

Then there was Dagger. He was an outdoor dog who looked like he would have much preferred to be in Alaska. With his wolfish features and swift, weightless speed, he could have easily pulled a sled across the vast tundra. The day we met him, he approached Cocoa, but despite Mama, Matt, and my sweet coaxing, he stayed away from us.

The woods were filled with knee-high snow, confining us to the cleared roads, so we regularly passed by Dagger's property. Most often, he would run ahead with Cocoa. He slowly warmed up to our appearance, acknowledging us with a high yip-howl and prancing as if he was a pivoting soccer player. Finally, he came close enough to sniff Mama's outreached hand, gaining trust, and then allowed us to pat him. It was like he was learning affection from humans for the first time.

Dagger would follow us home occasionally, perusing the yard with Cocoa. One chilly afternoon as Mama and I headed indoors, we turned to see him trailing us. A protective Cocoa didn't want him to invade her territory, perhaps she knew she would have to share her treats. She barked loudly after him, but he avoided her and darted inside, scooting under the table and by the wooden post.

Cocoa was already beside me, expecting my visit to the biscuit jar. She looked at Dagger anxiously, anticipating him to want a treat, but he ignored the offer. She was quite pleased as she gobbled hers. I sat on the floor, and Dagger lapped up the attention while Cocoa glared but left him alone. I rifled through her toy box, but neither of the dogs were interested. Dagger just stood staring at Mama and me, going back and forth getting pats from us. Cocoa settled under the table, resting her head on her paws, and I crawled over to give her a peck on her nose. I knew she was okay with us sharing our love.

Much to our surprise one morning, we walked by Dagger's house to see it was completely absent of any life. The random lawn clutter that had been strewn around was gone, as was the grill on the side deck and the kennels in the backyard. No lights were on, and the driveway was empty. The most meaningful loss was Dagger. He was nowhere to be found.

Cocoa went onto the property, sniffing the area with no sounds of objection from the previous inhabitants. We continued along the road, Cocoa seemingly saddened by the disappearance of her friend. The family had been evicted, and we never saw Dagger again. If only they had left him behind so he could still run wild in the woods. Maybe he had gone someplace with that same freedom.

Just when one loss was felt, a new character emerged. Mossie was a blundering bundle of pure energy. Cocoa positioned herself into a playful stance, ready to pounce when the strong black lab rumbled down the back path. Mossie had a long string of saliva dangling from the side of his mouth, and as he and Cocoa frolicked, it swung upward and stuck onto the top of his head. He ran toward me and I reached out to pat him, but Cocoa growled and intercepted his contact.

Mama opened the door, and he charged over to her. A deep voice hollered through the woods, "Mossie! Come home!" He looked around apprehensively and circled us before obeying the third call, his shock collar beeping as he thundered up the path and vanished into the dim glow of twilight. Mossie's visits were like that — loud, short, and full of boldness until he surrendered to his owner's command.

Cocoa loved his attention. She waited for him at the intersection of the back paths in the early evening hours, her gaze of anticipation focused uphill. When the neighbor's noisy truck banged along the road and his door slammed, her interest peaked as her friend came into view and they reunited once more.

Another winter visit and another big storm. It was the perfect opportunity to build a snowman again. I went outside and started forming the first ball. Cocoa raced up to it and took a big bite out of the side. I laughed and grabbed a handful of snow to fill the hole, smoothing the surface neatly. "Oh, you funny bunny," I said. She broke into her familiar high-pitched barking until I chucked a snowball for her to chase. My level of patience was decreasing when she quickly returned, repeating her protest.

Cocoa's loudness bounced off the trees. I threw a few more snowballs to distract her from my project, but she was onto me and merely watched them fall as she barked incessantly. "Cocoa, STOP!" I heard myself shout, but she didn't. My ears were ringing and I felt my irritation peak. Mama stepped out to join us. "Mama, she's really annoying me right now," I whined. "I just want to build a snowman!"

"I know… You know how she is," she answered. "Come on, Cokie." She made a snowball and threw it to her. I tried one last time to finish the base of the snowman, but she barked obstinately in my face.

"I give up," I said, feeling perturbed. "Thanks anyway, Mama." I needed to go for a walk and strapped on a pair of snowshoes. Cocoa was right by my side. She looked at me and jumped up lightly on her front paws. "We're only going up to the field," I said grumpily.

We reached the first clearing, and Cocoa stuck her nose into deer tracks that led deep into the pine forest. I could feel the windburn on my face while I took in the overcast sky. The woods were silent. I peered ahead at Cocoa, her blond pantaloons swaying with her gait, and she glanced back, her eyes confirming her watchful lead. Why had I gotten so frustrated? I loved her colorful personality. She was sweet, stubborn, and adventurous, yet I had lost my patience with her. I had been away for over a year, got married, was trying to live a "grown up" life… And then it hit me. Had I hardened in doing so? Was I taking life too seriously? Had I lost some of my passion because of this?

I stared at the glistening snow as the clouds parted for the sun. The sparkles across the open field looked like little diamonds — treasures — their bright reflections forcing me to squint. The cold wind picked up, and the sun was hidden once again. I was gazing at a stark winterscape. In that moment, I realized the beauty that had been revealed to me was exactly what my eyes needed to take in. Then, with simply a change of lighting and perspective, it was hidden. Masked. But it was always there.

When we got home, Cocoa and I stayed outside together. I made an entire snow family including a dog while Cocoa barked happily, expressing her presence, her company. I had just forgotten how joyful she made me feel, like diamonds on the snow.

I heard Mama putting away the dishes in the kitchen and went downstairs for breakfast. Cocoa ran to greet me, licking my face and making me laugh as I dropped to the floor and hugged her tightly. This affection would have to sustain me for another year or so until I saw her next. Mama smiled. "Morning. The water has boiled if you want tea," she said.

"Morning!" I prepared a cup and sat at the table before realizing that Cocoa was missing. I scanned the living room.

"She's probably on my bed," Mama answered my unsaid question. Sure enough, I found her curled up in the warm sheets. I snuggled beside her and brushed my fingers through her coat. Her eyes recognized what pained me to admit — I had to leave her again. A tear rolled down my cheek as I felt like I was betraying her, like I was betraying a part of myself.

We walked the snowy road to the pond, the back paths too deep to move through. Cocoa was in the lead, as always. I kicked a pine cone, and she turned to stop it. I was trying to be cheerful, but our conversations were hushed by the anticipation of saying goodbye. I skidded along the ice patches in the short section of forest before the field with an unobstructed view of Ragged Mountain.

It stood out in its plain winter beauty, covered with trees that appeared gray and muted from this distance. Matt pointed his camera at the scene. The guttural clicking of crows caught our attention when we rounded the bend. They were everywhere, lining the branches like ornamental leaves. But despite their number, they became peculiarly still and silent while we passed. Cocoa looked up uneasily and broke into a run as one suddenly unfolded his wings and flew overhead.

Nearing the end of the road, it was clear that many had attempted a path toward the pond but stopped just as the frozen masterpiece came into sight. "I'm definitely going down there," I said, taking charge to forge the rest of the path in the shin-deep snow. My position didn't last long as Cocoa rushed by, plowing through it with full leaps. She knew what awaited us below.

"Careful of the tree roots," I called to Mama and Matt, who were following in our tracks. The pond was a plush white field, and with the soft hue of the sky, it had a cozy feeling about it. A wall of drifted snow and ice was at the front of the boathouse, with icicles hanging from the eaves. I pulled one down. Cocoa grabbed it from my hand like it was a big stick and pranced into the building with her new possession.

I chipped away at the mounded pile of layered snow, repeatedly planting my heel until I broke off a sizeable piece. Cocoa was ecstatic. "Let's play!" I said as she shook, her body unable to contain her excitement. "Back it up!" Mama and Matt joined us in the boathouse as I threw the snow puck onto the floor. Cocoa pounced, and our game of ice hockey began.

The lens clicked as Matt captured pictures of us. "Switch sides!" I yelled. Mama stood next to me, kicking frozen chunks across the floor in Cocoa's direction. I pretended to dribble a basketball and did a lay-up to the rafters and she jumped to block me, boxing me out with skilled athleticism. "Okay, take a break," I said. Cocoa sunk her nose into the snow and chewed a mouthful before strolling over to Matt as he observed Ragged Mountain from a new angle. This was the way I wanted to spend our last morning at home — out in the elements appreciating the simple glory of being with my beloved companions.

I was on the phone with Mama. She was overjoyed. "I went outside to brush the snow off my jeep and saw something flying toward us…"

"What was it?" My imagination was going wild.

"I couldn't tell at first. Then it got close enough and landed on a branch of the maple tree. I was staring into the eyes of a Great Gray Owl!"

"Wow, that's so cool!"

"Cocoa just sat there studying him, not flinching a muscle. His eyes were the same yellow as hers, and he looked back and forth at us while I spoke to him. We were out there for a few minutes before he finally spread his wings and was gone as quickly as he had come."

"Maybe he was bringing a message to you?" I wondered.

"Yes! It was like he purposefully came to see us, like he already knew us. I read in my bird book that they are quite rare in these parts, so I feel pretty special to have had the privilege of his company." I was intrigued as we talked about the marvelous encounter. Nature always had a way of delivering signs to us, whether or not we were aware of it. There was definitely meaning to the owl's visit.

And we were off, just like always, as if no time had passed. Cocoa welcomed me with so much love and seeming understanding, but I couldn't quite fathom that I was deserving of this treatment. Was it forgiveness or simply acceptance of what was? I chose to leave her for "more," and I now realized that maybe *she* was my more.

The trips home came and went, some Matt joined me on, while others I was alone. When unaccompanied, we would let days, even a week go by before contacting each other. We were together but separate, and sometimes it felt like a dream that I had settled down in a land so far away. I considered it a freedom that I could still maintain my independence.

My siblings were busy with their own lives and experiences, and there were many people to catch up with. I adored meeting my nieces and nephews. They inspired me. I looked forward to my visits with Paw, when I could bring him into my world of dreaming. I told him of my struggles and fears, but also of my hopes and aspirations. All along, Mama continued to cheer me on, encouraging, supporting, and believing in me.

Closest to my heart was returning to the woods where I would be enveloped in nature with Cocoa by my side. This was when I could strip myself of identity and just "be." Every expectation I had would dissipate into the fresh air, my senses heightened from being an observer of the surroundings, encompassing me as one. I could easily get lost in that tranquility of being. Those days seemed to linger on through each seamless moment until the anxiety about a less-perfect world of obligatory structure crept in, and I had to say goodbye once again.

I was in Sydney with Melina, and we were on the ferry to Manly Beach. As the vessel turned direction, the sea breeze blew my hair against my tear-stained skin. I had just gotten a call from Katie. Mama had slipped on black ice at work and landed on her head. She was in the hospital. I felt the blood drain from my face, my breath in my throat. Melina rushed to my side. "What happened?" It took me a minute to formulate the words. I was utterly helpless and couldn't register or focus on anything. My dear friend comforted me.

I heard my phone beep with a message updating me that Mama was awake and conscious, and I could call her. The busy environment of Manly Beach froze until I heard her speak. "I'm okay," Mama said, somehow injecting cheerfulness into her weak voice. Movement and life around me picked up once again. "I'm probably going to have black eyes, though!" she joked.

"Oh, Mama, I was so worried. I feared the worst," I told her, tears streaming down my cheeks.

"I know, Amandy."

"I wish I could be there right now," I spoke through sniffles.

"I know, but I'll just be resting. Really, I'll be okay," Mama reassured me. A nurse needed her attention and I said goodbye, feeling both relief and frustration. I found out later that the scans showed she had damage to her cervical spine. It was going to be a long road to recovery.

I didn't realize the extent of Mama's throbbing pain, the constant vertigo she suffered with accompanying paresthesia. As weeks passed, it was one thing after another. But she was adamant that she'd get better with minimal treatment, working through her physical therapy and resting as much as possible. Cocoa was by her side all the while.

The politics that came along with the liability of her workplace brought about unnecessary stress that slowed her healing. She was not only trying to recover from such a traumatic incident, she was made to feel like it was *her* fault. That the unsanded sidewalk was of no consequence. After my accident, I could relate to some degree, although Mama went through this for almost a year following a much more severe injury. Yet again, I searched for the justice in it.

She now had to advocate for herself, and as always, she persevered. I believed it was her continued optimism and faith that helped her through the hardest parts. That, and being in the refuge of home with her tremendously loyal canine companion. Mama's fall was a wake-up call to me — a heart-stopping reminder that things would happen whether or not I was living back home. Life would happen. For as many good things that would occur, there would eventually be the balance I so feared to think. *All we really have is right now.*

CHAPTER TEN:

Home Again

I sat on the balcony, staring out at the panoramic view of the ocean. It was a flawlessly sunny Easter. Kayaks, paddle boards, and boats dotted the water, and the surf could be heard in the distance. Despite the beauty, I felt sadness, tears filling my eyes as I absorbed the news. My father was in the hospital, very sick with an infection severe enough for the doctors to be concerned. It was the unsaid knowing in the back of our minds that there would come a day when Paw's disease would take its final toll and his fight would be over. It now appeared the time had come, and this would be the trip home I feared.

⇀

I took my window seat on the plane, hoping that no one would be sitting next to me. The last thing I was in the mood for was small talk. I had three seats to myself when the flight attendants started checking the passengers. Behind them was a man approaching my row. He nodded at me. "Hi." I greeted him with a smile, and he took the aisle seat. *Why did he look so familiar?* I snuck glances at him. His bushy eyebrows, his soft blue eyes, his cherub-like skin... He resembled Paw. I turned to the window with tears in my eyes as I knew there was no such thing as coincidences.

The sun streamed through my window as we ascended high above the very same water I had been staring at the day before. The man sat quietly during the trip, and my attention drifted to Paw. I thought of the prison he had been living in for so long, the inability to express himself when he was once a talented musician, a sensitive artist who became disheartened by the hard aspects of reality. For most of my life, he battled diseases in his body, from addiction to chronic illness. I hadn't been able to get to know who he was outside of that. I settled into the long journey, wanting sleep to take its course so my mind could rest.

James picked me up from the airport. "I told Paw I had no doubt that you'd come home," he said. If that offered our father even a spark of happiness, I was glad for it. I sat quietly while my brother shared his insights to help prepare me for the day to come.

On our way to the hospital, we stopped for a quick visit with Katie. She lived nearby and was on maternity leave. "Okay, where is he?" I asked. She motioned to the living room, and I went straight to the crib to meet her infant son, Alexander, and held him close. He was so tiny, so precious, and so incredibly vulnerable. Here was this being with stories yet to be made, and I was about to see Paw, whose new stories would soon come to an end. As devastating as it was to think of losing him, it was inevitable and almost beautifully poetic the way life gives and takes, like the ebb and flow of the tide.

I met Amaliya and Mama at the end of the corridor in the Intensive Care Unit, just outside of Paw's room. We shared hugs before I was instructed to put on a hospital gown and sanitize my hands. I walked toward my father. "Hi, Paw!" I tried to sound as cheerful as I could and smiled weakly. Taken by surprise, his gaze moved to me. "I needed to be here to see you again," I said, my tears brimming when I hugged him. "I'm so sorry you're going through this."

His eyes told me his condition. He was in pain but still holding on. I sat there for a while, feeling like I had a hundred things to say but found myself speechless. I followed his focus to the afternoon sun pushing through the gloomy sky to illuminate the trees, wondering what he was thinking. Mama came over. "We need to stay to talk with the doctors. Do you think you could drive the jeep home and be with Cokie?" She didn't have to ask me twice.

In the face of the sadness that brought me home was the joy of seeing my favorite companion, and our reunion was as it always had been — an outpouring of crying, wiggling, and uncapped happiness. For as big as she was, she still curled into my lap like a puppy. I rested my head on her torso and wrapped my arms around her, feeling tremendous peace and love.

"Cokie, Paw is very sick," I said, "and Mama is at the hospital with him." She stared at me with intense concentration before asking to be let outside. I knew what would be uplifting for both of us. "Do you want to go for a walk?" She jumped forward excitedly as I went to the door.

She seemed to be moving slower than usual, maybe she was tired or out of shape. I knew what a painful process of healing it had been for Mama since her fall, and the winter brought a recurring challenge as to when and where she walked. All the while, she told me Cocoa would stay beside her, wait when she was lagging, listen to her read chapter books, and give her all the kisses in the world "just because."

That afternoon, we ran the paths in the lingering snow. It was dismal and chilly, but that didn't matter. I felt my lungs open, life coursing through my body as I looked out at Ragged Mountain. My bear-like sidekick meandered along the shoreline of the pond, pausing to check on me, and I was whole again. It was without question that we were a team.

―

I headed to the local florist for a plant to liven up Paw's bleak hospital room. A potted pine stood out right away. Maybe it would remind him of the little tree he and Mama made for their first Christmas in the cabin. It could bring back a pleasant memory, a piece of the woods. I decorated the pot with ceramic figurines of woodland creatures, then went into my bag of meditation tools. I took out the crystals to encourage peace, love, and healing, burying a clear quartz in the soil and placing a purple amethyst and rose quartz around the base.

A nurse was checking Paw's vitals and smiled when I walked in. "You must be one of his daughters," she said. I returned her smile.

"Yes. I'm Amanda. I flew in last night."

"I've heard all about you — you live in Australia!" Paw opened his eyes, and I looked over to meet his gaze.

"That's me," I said. "I wish it wasn't so far from here, though."

The nurse was kind, and I was glad she was taking care of my father. "I have a cup of ice chips for your dad. You just swab them. They give him some moisture because his mouth is very dry." She demonstrated for me, and I observed Paw's relief.

"Thank you," I said softly, tears forming as I processed the fact that he couldn't consume anything without the risk of aspirating. She gave me a sympathetic nod and put her hand on my shoulder before leaving the room. Paw stared at me as I quickly brushed away my tears.

"I brought you this lovely pine tree." I set it on the table near the window. "Oxygen and ambience! I've also put crystals in the soil." I pointed out the purple amethyst and rose quartz. "These have healing properties." He turned to look out the window, then at me. "Want some music?" I shuffled through a pile of CDs to find Bonnie Raitt and cranked up the volume to our favorite song.

I sang as Paw watched me. He wanted so much to say something, and I prayed for him to be able to. *Just let it happen. Please, God*, I begged. His beautiful blue eyes were filled with frustration and disillusionment. I held his hand, briefly moving my thumb from side to side like when we used to play "Thumbs." I couldn't remember the last time he was willingly able to move his. The years had passed and so much had been stripped from him. How much suffering can one endure?

I took out my phone to show him the videos I had taken from the plane. He had never flown before, and as the sunlight cast heavenly beams through the clouds, I wanted him to notice. I moved the screen to his face, but he couldn't focus on it, his stare moving back toward the window. As the white noise from the flight played, I observed his eyes and suddenly understood that he didn't need to see the video.

I believed he would soon witness something more brilliant and light, maybe he was already starting to. I moved closer to him. "Paw, I know I've always told you to hold onto hope and that miracles happen if you just believe. I'm sorry that they didn't in the way we wanted. But you can be free. You will be free. Your miracle *will* come." His eyes were different now, almost relaxed. "We'll be okay, don't worry." I hugged him tightly.

While Mama and Nana sat with him that afternoon, I took out my singing bowl and began to play. Paw's drooping eyelids popped open with interest. I explained what it was and kept playing, walking around the bed so he could feel the sound vibrations. As he drifted off to sleep, I played softer and slower until the tone stopped.

I glanced at Mama, who was speaking to the nurse I had met. Her face was attentive, concerned, and in the light of difficult decisions, she stood strong, holding it all together once again. Beside her during the hospice meeting, I stared at the representative speaking, trying my best to follow every detail, every explanation, without letting my emotion overpower me. I knew Mama had something greater helping her to cope. Was it her faith in God?

Paw was taken by ambulance to his residential care home a week later. His health seemed to improve enough for an outing, and Mama organized for him to return home to the woods where our family would gather. He arrived on that spring morning, his life so obviously fading. He stared at the woods, his family, and gazed at his newest grandson so not to forget him. He briefly looked at the cabin he and Mama had built long ago.

As the children ran about, I watched Cocoa walk over to Paw and quietly wait by him. Pizza was put on the picnic table for lunch, but it felt wrong to have food around when he couldn't eat. I went to sit with him, trying to make eye contact, but I saw that he was somewhere else. He had already left the woods.

We found out from the staff at Paw's home that he had contracted MRSA in the hospital, and they went through the preventative measures so it wouldn't be passed to us. I was angry that I couldn't even hold his hand now without the fear of infection. That I could be denied offering comfort and support to him in his final moments. Regardless, I took his hand in mine.

"Okay," I said, "one more song." With just the two of us in the room, I sang with all the energy I could muster up, then gave him a hug, my ear on his chest. His heartbeat was so fast, like a freight train in full gear. I put my hand on his face. "Thank you, Paw. I love you." As visitors came into the room, I headed toward the door, looking back at my father for the last time.

Hours passed and Mama came home to get a change of clothes and some toiletries before joining Paw again. "Thank you, Amandy," she said.

"No problem at all. You know I'll be here with Cokie. Take care…" Words wouldn't suffice for the degree of agony that was ahead. I gave her a big hug and she left. The night went by. Cocoa and I slept soundly until the glowing moon suddenly woke me.

I fumbled for the phone. It was 7:30 a.m. and James' voice told me Paw didn't have much longer. "If you want to see him, this is your last chance," he said. I *had* seen him. Enough pain. Enough was enough.

"No, James, stay there." An hour later he called.

"He's gone."

I looked outside at the sunny, cheerful morning and saw a robin land on a branch. Scanning the front yard, I noticed there were birds everywhere, singing loudly and joyfully. "You're free, Paw," I said with relief. *Free as one of these birds*. But then I had so many questions. *Where have you gone? Are you still with*

Mama and James in the room? What is it like? Are you drifting? Is it light? Is it beautiful? Are you in the woods? Are you everywhere?* I became unsettled in wondering before I stopped myself. "You are free," I concluded. Cocoa's eyes met mine, and I felt confident. Maybe that was all the answer I needed.

Everything happened quickly after Paw's death. Mama and I returned to his room and went through all of his belongings, taking down the framed photo collages that chronicled our family throughout the years. Mama folded his clothes, bagging the ones she wanted to save, and decided on what he would be buried in.

"I was thinking of this." She held up a black short-sleeved shirt with Steely Dan on the front.

"That's perfect, exactly what he would want. What do you think about the plaid flannel shirt over it? It's at home in my closet."

"That was one of his favorites," she said quietly.

"It'll fit him unbuttoned, and there's a chest pocket if anyone wants to leave a note or memento." Mama nodded at my suggestion and pointed out the glass doors to the backyard. It was a beautiful day.

"A robin landed there shortly after he died," she said. I exhaled in silent understanding of yet another sign.

We needed to organize the services and burial details. The funeral director sat opposite us, a gentle giant of a man with a sincere nature. "I know there's a lot to consider. If you follow me, you can see the caskets I have. There are also catalogues with others that can be shipped here," he said.

How disturbing. I had never been in a showroom of caskets, and this was the first time I processed death as a business. We walked around the room in silence. The displays seemed extravagant and way too expensive. "Paw wouldn't want any of these," my mother said.

"How about we sit down and look in the catalogues?" I grabbed one and flipped through the pages until we came upon some craftsman styles, simple but impressive, honoring the trees they were made from.

"This one," she decided, then broke into tears. It was all too much to absorb. "I haven't even been able to grieve…" In the heaviness of sorrow, I needed to be *her* fortress now. We waited together in that space until a wave of strength helped us to carry on.

The florist pulled into the yard again with another flower arrangement. A dozen had been delivered in the past few days from family and friends. As their sweet perfumes filled the air, we went through the family albums. The music that Mama and Paw shared with us over the years was playing, and we sat reminiscing.

Cocoa continually comforted Mama, standing close, offering to be hugged. "Oh, Cokie, you just *know*," she said, embracing her tightly. The picture she had been holding fell onto her lap, and she placed it back on the table. As we created the photo collage for the wake, I stared at each memory, so many of them illustrated such goofiness, such love. I looked at my father's expressions and thought, *Wow, what a life. What a story.*

The next day was very cold. In the face of a bitter wind, Mama and I went to the cemetery and picked out the only plot available near a tree. It wasn't far off the busy main road. "We'll be able to see his tombstone when we drive by," Mama said.

"It's a great spot," I agreed, imagining the tree in full bloom come springtime.

Mama had a loving smile on her face as she peered down at Cocoa. "She's licking the lotion off my legs," she laughed. I grinned. Cocoa moved to give her attention to me as if knowing I held something special in my hands.

"I've been working on my eulogy. Can I read it to you?" Mama nodded and I took a deep breath. It was written with a brief section of singing, but as I tried rehearsing, the notes got stuck in my throat. I knew I would have to skip these parts if I was too emotional.

"That's very heartfelt," Mama said when I finished. Cocoa rested her chin on my leg, and I slid onto the floor with her, smoothing her silky coat.

"When I was going through pictures, I found some letters Nana had given me years ago," Mama said, disappearing into her room and returning with a stack of envelopes. "I've never read them."

I was intrigued as she set them in the middle of the table. She reached for the first one and started to read it out loud. It was from my father as a young college student writing to his mother and grandmother. He told them about school and that he liked it, but he couldn't wait to travel, speaking of his plans to visit his aunt and uncle in Florida, then to go out west. His tone was excited, optimistic of what was to come after graduation.

As Mama and I swapped turns reading a new letter, Paw's character became all the more familiar as he cheerfully detailed his latest adventures. He had taken the trip down to Florida, slept near the ocean, played guitar around campfires and under the stars, and continued west. He crossed a section of the Rio Grande River in Mexico in "The Blue Goose" truck he refurbished, worked on a family farm for little money, and used his carpentry skills in Texas. All the while, he was sending most of his earnings home to pay for his college loans. He didn't live on much, but he had freedom in that.

Paw mentioned the latest album by the band America, saying how it really spoke to him, especially the song "Ventura Highway." He was so poetic in his accounts, wanting to help the beautiful Mexican children with "tanned skin and sun-blistered lips." He had dreams of building a church for them to give hope of a brighter future, and he trusted his faithful mother would be proud of him.

He painted pictures with his words, and it was like we were there with him. But for as upbeat as he sounded, I could hear that same questioning, that same fragility, self-doubt, and fear of settling into a world governed by excessiveness, where the simple beauties of life appeared forgotten. I wished I could speak with him, to share how I felt many of the things he had.

I stared at the last envelope on the table. "Your turn," I said to Mama, my eyesight blurred with tears. "I don't want them to end." I was learning a lot about who my father once was. After the final letter had been read, we sat together in silent gratitude.

It dawned on me that those many times I had described my own struggles to him, Paw understood exactly how I felt despite his inability to vocalize it. The adamant look in his eyes confirmed he had been actively relating with me all along, and I was not alone in this experience. What a gift bestowed upon us to have read those letters at that chosen moment.

I scrolled through my iPod to the song he had noted. The sound filled the room. I closed my eyes and imagined the reel of his stories playing — the beach where he saw the sunrise on the water, the highway, making music as the weight of the world disappeared, the vastness of the starry sky, the adventure, the dreaming.

The line of people attending the wake extended far out the door. The casket was now closed after our private family viewing, and I was relieved. The body inside was merely a shell. Paw had moved out of it, and it was startlingly clear as I recalled staring down at him, not recognizing the face so frozen, devoid of the very thing that made my father. Still, I put the paw pendant I had made for him into the pocket of his flannel shirt. I touched his cold hand and kissed his cheek. "I love you, Paw," I said out loud. He must have heard me somewhere, but where? Where had his light gone?

The funeral was held in the little church my family attended regularly during my childhood. The casket rested in the middle of the aisle in front of the altar, and I couldn't shake the distinct feeling that it was empty. We gathered during the priest's blessing, and I watched the smoke from the incense dissipate. It was so strange with only six of us together. *What a monumental presence a single being can have.* As the service began, my niece Ailyn sat beside me, cheerful and light in her demeanor. She reminded me that everything was okay.

My mother did the first reading, her voice filled with courage as she eloquently spoke. Then, along with my four siblings and Paw's best friend, Joe, we stood up to deliver our own thoughts. It was enlightening to get a glimpse of each unique perspective. When my turn came, I approached the lectern and unfolded my piece of notebook paper.

I faced everyone and somehow felt incredibly strong. From somewhere within me, I summoned my most powerful refrain from Bonnie Raitt's song. I looked at Mama, a warm smile on her face and so much love exuding from her angelic aura. I spoke briefly, then ended on a high note with "Over the Rainbow." I couldn't believe that I had delivered it exactly how I wanted to, in honor of my father. And I knew I had help — that a light had been with me. Everything *was* okay.

As we said goodbye to Paw's body at the burial, the frigid wind seemed to push us toward the warmth and comfort of the reception. Every past family gathering had been filled with that kind of warmth through shared company and music. I put on "Ventura Highway" and smiled, turning up the volume to fill every space. It was as if my father was in the hall with us. James took out Paw's electric guitar as Ben and our cousin Jake started playing piano. Nana joined in, then Jake played his accordion. This was it. *This* was a worthy celebration of life.

The next morning, I heard Mama talking and opened my window. "Look out at the garden," she said. There was a beautiful doe standing near the corner of it, staring at her. "Paw sent you to give me a message. Oh, thank you so much," Mama acknowledged. I watched as the majestic animal waited calmly, locked in eye contact before finally stirring, her tail flicking up as she leapt off. Cocoa had been only ten feet away but was as motionless as the doe.

For some reason, I was compelled to grab my camera and went outside, taking photos of the garden, the flowers Mama had planted, the old milk can, the garden gnome, and the rustic scenery. As I went through them later, I noticed something odd in one picture. I zoomed in and saw a cloud-like manifestation hovering over the entrance to the back paths. *It's Paw!* I thought, sending the image to my siblings. James called soon after.

"That's exactly where he used to sit and whistle to the birds," he said.

⁓

I had always found cemeteries interesting. I could spend hours studying gravestones with names, dates, and messages about the deceased, left behind for loved ones and strangers alike to remember or gather just a tiny piece of their stories. I knew Paw's would certainly deliver that with a caption from one of our shared favorites, "The Road Not Taken" by Robert Frost.

Holly and I would often walk through the old cemetery down the street, over a scrappy bridge and murky creek to the fields. One day, I came across a pathway leading around the perimeter and was instantly curious. "Holly, come on, girl!" I coaxed her toward me with the frisbee in my hand. She didn't like to go to unfamiliar places, but this time she followed.

Vines hung low and I dodged a few spider webs as the path turned rough. Some of the gravestones on the edge were so weathered that they were indecipherable. Artificial flowers adorned numerous sites, while the cement that topped others was cracked and exposed the earth beneath. A tree grew out of another. I loved the symbolism, for many years ago, I planted a hydrangea on top of Lady's grave for that greater meaning of a body growing into more.

Holly found something appetizing and crunched on it before the pathway ended. We ventured down a slope to a small wooded area where a graffitied park bench sat. I had seen it from a distance but never envisioned it was amidst this accessible pocket of forest. I looked ahead for snakes in the leaf debris, and a bush turkey startled me as he ran by, squawking at our presence.

There was a break in the trees, and Holly picked up a scent along the narrow trail. For a minute, I couldn't tell where we were. It smelled of decomposing leaves, transporting me to the feeling of fall in New Hampshire. It was like being embraced by a masked suburbia.

I sit on the veranda, sipping tea and staring out at the bountiful tree. A family of crows have landed in it. I watch them. One stares straight at me, and I am mesmerized by his dark feathers glinting a shimmery green in the sun. He seems all-knowing. My mind drifts back to the crows in the stark winter in the woods, and I am drawn to write as I process new thoughts, new emotions about my life.

I reflected on my conversation with the stranger on the boardwalk. After all the years that had passed, the trips back and forth, the emotional hurdles, my mother's trauma, and the loss of my father, I began to grasp and identify with each moment for what it was. In doing this, something amazing started to happen. I was seeing Australia the way I first did.

I took charge of my own healing and stopped limiting myself in doing the things I loved to do. I ceased worrying about so much — the sun, heat, city-living, creepy crawlers... I realized that I was using them as excuses not to accept my new home. I joined a hiking group, investigated scenic parks, and for the first time in ages, I consistently wrote. I sang, twirled, and danced with joy. I began to meditate regularly and sought out ways to self-develop, considering different spiritual concepts.

As heart-wrenching as it was to leave Cocoa, I knew that when I saw her again during my next visit to the woods, we would share the most precious greeting, the same love and companionship, and even bigger adventures together. That, indeed, would not change. My tears in leaving didn't last as long as I was consoled by this, my heart open as I focused only on the continued love — the love of spending time with Cocoa, then the love in returning to Holly. I was discovering how to be truly present.

And things kept on shifting. I was seeing the light. The battle I had once been in was over, and I understood that I had to make peace and be content with who I was. In doing so, happiness filled my life in more ways. I was recognizing that I had the best of both worlds. I *could* have two homes and so much love for each of them.

CHAPTER ELEVEN:

Time Stops

A mad rush of devastation hit me when my mother answered the phone in a choked-up voice and told me the dreadful news. Cocoa had lymphoma, and the vet had given her three weeks to live. It felt like my body was suffocating, like a stone gavel had struck it in one blow that caused the light to seep out of me, my soul dying. I was crushed in every way but with no physical wounds, and nothing else mattered to me anymore.

I awoke that night, reminded of the fate of my innocent, beautiful best friend. My tears were so large and continuous, I just wanted to go into a deep and numbing sleep so all of this nightmare would disappear. It wasn't supposed to be this way. The unthinkable was happening, and I had no control. Immensely supportive, Matt knew I needed to go home to spend Cocoa's last moments with her.

During the long flight, I was suddenly optimistic and determined. I had started learning how to work with Reiki energy, and maybe I was led to it for this very reason. I kept photos of Cocoa close, jotting down notes from the *Reiki Shamanism* book I was reading, filling my journal with anything remotely suggestive of healing. Divine light energy, nature, crystals, sound therapy... I was intent on saving Cocoa.

I was desperate for her greeting. I ached for that emotional confirmation of our reunion. But when I got out of the truck, the predictable cries, wiggling bum, falling down, licks to my face — none of it happened. It was as if Cocoa didn't even know me. Something had clearly changed, and I couldn't comprehend it. I just wanted things to be the same again so her sickness didn't seem overpowering. So I felt like I had a fighting chance against it.

I stared out the window to see Cocoa lying on the ground. The frost was only beginning to soften its grip, but she loved the cold. She always had. Her body bulged in the center, a foreign leanness around her sides, and I watched the rise and fall of her breathing. I felt sad seeing her look so lost and alone. But then hope reignited. I opened the door, Cocoa barely acknowledging the sound, and went outside.

"Hi, Cokie," I said tenderly, squatting down to kiss the top of her head. She gazed at me with tired eyes. I kneaded my fingers through her coat, gently massaging her chest as she took in the chilly air, then rested my hands on her expanding torso. I could feel Reiki energy channeling through me, my hands getting warmer and warmer, tingling with power, and she let out a labored exhale and became very still. My calves were cramping as I held that pose for five, ten, fifteen minutes... I didn't really know. I just wanted to ease her pain. The chickadees chirped merrily and a chipmunk raced past us, but she didn't move.

Mama walked over with a blanket and draped it around me, then knelt to place her hands on Cocoa's face. She kissed her nose. "Thanks, Mama," I said, noticing her weak smile filled with desperation for hope. "I'm really feeling so much. My hands are hot and tingly — I haven't felt the energy this intense before!" Her distraught expression seemed to loosen.

"Really?" she asked, her eyes searching for optimism in my response.

"Yes! I think it's helping her!" There weren't any rainbows in the sky, but we both held onto the same hope. I still believed in more. That magic existed and miracles *could* happen. Cocoa got up soon after, and I understood that she'd had enough for now.

I wanted to create a comforting and easily accessible space for Cocoa. She no longer jumped up on the couches or beds. I looked around the downstairs living room and found the ideal place in the front right corner where the loveseat was. Close to the solar glass, it would be nice and cool there.

Mama was at the grocery store, so I had just enough time to reconfigure everything. Cocoa was lying on the carpet watching me. "I'm going to make you a cozy new spot!" I took her velveteen face in my hands and rubbed her cheeks before she moved to the kitchen.

Testing the weight of the loveseat, I walked it toward my body. It wasn't heavy but awkward with a bulky frame and puffy cushions. I shifted it along the floor and approached the bottom of the staircase, gripping the frame to pivot between the built-in shelving and the post.

"Come on, Saint Michael!" I cried, remembering Nana's story of trying to move a refrigerator, and a prayer to the archangel relocated it with ease. Adjusting my grip, I slowly backed up the stairs while pulling the loveseat by its side. Once at the top landing, it was too wide to fit through the door frame to the living room.

Cocoa waited at the bottom of the stairs. "Almost done, girl!" I unscrewed the legs and slid it across the floorboards, past the little red stove, positioning it next to the chaise lounge near the plants. *Phew!* It was a great addition to the garden-like area. I joined Cocoa and gave her a big hug. "Just a little more to go," I promised, putting down her plush new dog bed and rearranging the crystals I surrounded her with daily. "This is for you, girl!" I tapped the bed. She walked by it hesitantly, her eyes on the doorknob. I let her out only to hear a scratch seconds later — she wanted to come in.

"You're not sure where you want to be, huh, Cokie?" I went to the biscuit jar, grabbed a few treats, and sat on the footstool, holding my hands out for her to choose. I had done this countless times, but now I was extremely focused, taking note of her large auburn and white paws, the look of strength in them, the long tufts of white hair growing between her pads.

The delicacy of her touch was in complete contrast to her paws, noticeable when she tapped one of my fists lightly, then the other before heading over to the living room. She gave a sideways glance at the bed and continued on toward the big couch. I had an idea and grabbed some more biscuits, breaking them into halves. Cocoa's ears perked up.

"Want to play Hide and Seek?" I chose from the collection of stuffed animals my mother had displayed, scattering the monkey, brown bear, giraffe, white dog, elephant, leopard, gorilla, and bird across both couches. Cocoa was interested and certainly still loved this game.

"Wait, Cokie." I put my hand up as I placed the biscuit pieces randomly under the animals, saving a couple for the koala and Mr. Froggy, whom I situated on the new bed. She followed me, already nosing the animals and chewing her finds, and soon she was beside me. I caught her reluctant gaze. She was able to reach the koala from where she stood on the rug. "Check Mr.

Froggy," I said. Apprehensively, she took one step onto the bed and nosed her favorite toy to get the final biscuit of the game.

I could hear Mama coming down the driveway, and Cocoa was already at the door. "Who's here?!" Her tail bud slowly wiggled back and forth. The engine stopped and she broke into a light run to greet Mama, who gladly welcomed her into a hug. I smiled and gathered the grocery bags.

"I bought more whipped cream!" Mama said, handing me the canister.

"Ooohhh... Look, Cokie, whipped cream!" I sprayed three dollops into a bowl and put it on the floor for the keen recipient. "Come see the living room, Mama." Her eyes lit up.

"What a good place for Cocoa. But how did you move that loveseat all by yourself? It must have been heavy!" I grinned.

"Just a little awkward. It's upstairs." She was pleased with the relocation.

"I wanted some extra seating up here too," she said. "What a great fit!"

By that night, Cocoa still hadn't accepted her new bed. In an attempt to cheer her up, I sat at the piano and started playing her song. She whimpered, soon crooning out the notes in her beautiful singing voice. "Yay!" we applauded her. Right when we settled into the reconfigured space to watch television, she began pacing and glanced at the door.

I let her out and went downstairs to turn on the light, moving the curtain to see outside. There stood my lovely girl, staring at me. I giggled. "Come on in, cutie pie!" I gave her a mini biscuit before going upstairs with her in pursuit. "One sec," I told Mama, grabbing the hairbrush from my dresser.

When I returned to the living room, Cocoa was moving toward me, her latest marrow bone hanging halfway out of her mouth. She looked at me intently, almost making sure I was paying attention while she walked up to the loveseat and gently placed the bone on the cushion. Mama and I watched in amazement as she slowly lifted her front legs and climbed onto it to lie down, resembling a proud lioness reclaiming the spot she was not yet ready to relinquish. She didn't stay there long but was so obviously showing us she would lead the way on her own terms.

I constantly channeled Reiki for Cocoa. Her body calmed when I rested my hands on her, out in the chilly air or by the couch where I camped to be close. I visualized white light flooding her chakras, her body soothed and restored. But as much as I wanted her to get better, I knew deep down that my intent could not overpower what was her chosen path.

She became increasingly restless after her nightly dose of medication and preferred to be outside. Mama and I alternated turns taking her around the yard, luring her indoors with biscuits when it was just too cold. The temperatures continued to dip near freezing as winter lingered on.

The coydogs were particularly active and our protective instincts took over, knowing better than to leave Cocoa out on her own. Our fears were well-founded. I got up from the couch one night when the door slammed shut. "That was creepy," Mama said breathlessly.

"What happened?"

"I was shining the flashlight as Cokie went toward the back paths, moving the light ahead of her as she went, and saw three coydogs run by. They were not even ten feet away!"

"That's so scary," I said. "We'll have to be extra careful. They seem to be getting closer than usual."

The sky was dark and moonless. I walked outside with Cocoa and could see our breath under the stars. I pointed the flashlight in the direction she was headed, hoping she would pee, but instead she wandered down the hill, around the sinkholes and thorns, and into the woods. She turned, her eyes reflecting red with the light. "Cokie, come on, girl!" I called to her. *Where was she going?* She paused in consideration, looking past the garden before retracing her trail to me. Suddenly, I heard something running on the path by the outhouse to my right.

"Cokie!" I felt nervous, my heart thumping loudly. The sound was getting closer... Running from another direction now, more than one presence. I shined the light through the trees but couldn't see anything. I begged Cocoa to hurry, and fortunately, she picked up her pace and followed until we were safely inside. Closing the door behind us, the problems with the latch persisted. Finally after the fourth slam, it shut tightly.

"Everything okay?" Mama's voice came from her bedroom.

"I think the coydogs were here again," I said. "We might have to start leashing Cokie." Cocoa looked at me, unaffected by the close encounter. *What if she had somehow called in the coydogs? Perhaps she was trying to escape to the woods?* I had heard of pets who ventured into the wilderness to die, but I couldn't face these confronting speculations. I patted her and went to the biscuit jar, placing two treats in my fists for her to choose. She still had her appetite, so maybe she was healing?

Mama sat on the floor with Cocoa. I watched as she hid a treat under each piece of the wooden memory puzzle. Cocoa waited until she was given the word and pawed at the board, her rewards revealed one after another. "Cokie, what's this?" I said when she was done gobbling them up. I started playing my singing bowl. She walked up to it for a brief investigation, then eyed it suspiciously before asking to go outside. I shrugged at Mama.

Cocoa wasn't drinking a lot of water, but as usual, she loved to chomp on ice. We filled little bowls and set up stations around the house, frequently replenishing them and sometimes adding whipped cream as a treat. She was ravenous, so I took care in her meal preparations, hoping the boost of nutrition would give her the energy she needed. Although I had initially been positive that she still had an appetite, doubt crept into my mind as I began to fear we were only feeding the cancer.

I listened to Mama's phone conversation with the vet. We were desperate for ideas, anything to help her. I was using all I knew to ease her pain, but her discomfort was increasingly apparent. She was so advanced that any medical treatment had a minimal chance of success, and putting her through that would likely take away what quality time she had left, *we* had left together. I wasn't ready to let go, but was I bordering on selfishness and causing Cocoa to suffer?

"How will we know when she's had enough?" Mama asked.

"She'll make it clear to you," the vet said. "You'll know."

―

Sunlight falls on my face, and its warmth brings me home. The path was shady with patches of light hitting the leaves that Cocoa's paws slowly walked upon, leading us toward the lower section of rushing water and down the sloping hill covered with pine needles. I watched her as she traipsed onward, looking around as if memorizing the trees, the kiss of the afternoon glow, the current's swirls and ripples, the random rocks... We stopped at the base of the hill and found a log to sit on as Cocoa carefully waded into the brook, putting her nose to the surface in an effort to blow bubbles as always. I felt the warm sun on my skin and closed my eyes, caressed by the uplifting star.

Mama's voice called to Cocoa and she navigated upstream across from us but stayed in the water. Maybe it revitalized her. She paused, almost statuesque as her eyes were locked in an unfocused gaze. A cloud passed overhead and she snapped out of it, dipping her nose into the water again and blowing bubbles this time before joining us on land. A young dog appeared, trailed by a woman, and ran to Cocoa. After a brief interaction, she became indifferent and stared at me for the last biscuit in my pocket.

"Wanna go for a walk, Cokie?" Her ears perked up. I knew she wanted to see her friend again and maybe the pond. Walking the beginning of the back path, she stopped in her tracks and looked at us reluctantly. It was too much of an endeavor to go on foot. "How about a ride?" I said. She happily strode to Mama's new car and I helped her onto the seat.

Suka gladly welcomed her, and the two wandered the yard. "Hey!" Barb emerged from the side of the house. "How's Cocoa doing?"

"She's slowing down but still has interest in things," I said.

"It's a day at a time," Mama added in a hopeful tone. Cocoa greeted Barb affectionately before Suka stole her attention as he went near the gathering of farm animals. I watched the friends side by side and couldn't fathom that it had been over eight years since they had first met here as puppies. Now they stood together, seemingly closer than ever.

There were leftover acorns scattered about. Just as I went to pick one up, Cocoa was in front of me, anticipating the throw.

We couldn't play pine cone hockey at the boathouse or the rock game at the shoreline of the pond, but she still had the energy for acorns. Her body quivered as she caught, chomped, and let them fall. Like sweet music to my ears, her high-pitched bark melted my heart.

A car drove up the road, diverting our attention. Ben and his sons, Logan and Hunter, had come for a visit. Cocoa watched as we played outside, got kindling, and filled the wheelbarrow with wood. I ran to her, my eyes searching hers until Hunter let out a little squeal. He had noticed the big plastic ball by the garden. I rolled it his way and he smiled, pushed it back to me, and the game went on.

From the corner of my eye, I could see Cocoa prancing toward me. She was the happiest I had seen her during my return home. Her eager eyes directed me to follow her past some saplings to a wooded section next to the shed. "What is it, Cokie?" She studied a mound of leaves at the base of a small oak tree.

I immediately understood what she was pointing out — she had hidden a bone for me to find. Her warm yellow eyes brightened and she looked at me, then tipped her chin to the mound. I reached into the leaves and sifted through them, but much to my surprise, nothing else was there. "Where is it, girl?" She put her nose to the ground and nudged the soil, instructing me to dig.

I scooped the damp earth, combing it aside, and finally exposed the white of her marrow bone. Her bum wiggled cheerfully. "Yay, Cokie! I found it!" I brushed away the dirt before giving her the prized possession. "That was awesome! What a great hiding place. Oh, thank you, girl!" I hugged her tightly.

Her energy kept up as she charged off. I could hardly contain my delight when she paused to inspect the landscape, scoping out a new hiding spot, the bone casually hanging from her mouth. She looked at me as if to check that I wasn't cheating, and I quickly turned, pretending I hadn't seen her. A couple minutes later, she pranced back to get me, clearly ready for the next round.

I felt giddy as I followed her lead to the rocks that formed the fire pit. Her excavation was evident, and I knelt down to shovel into the dirt, her eyes expectantly wanting me to continue the game. More digging uncovered the recognizable object. I smiled. "Guys, Cokie is playing Hide and Seek with me!" Mama observed the big hole where the bone had just been.

"Wow, you're so smart!" She petted Cocoa, who then took off to another spot. She made this one difficult, indicating toward a towering pile of debris behind the raised garden bed. I swept through it, but the bone was nowhere to be found.

"Where is it?" I asked. She pawed some leaves aside. "Hmmm, where could it be?" I watched her search until a ball rolling over distracted me. Hunter and Mama waited for my throw, and Cocoa found the bone in the interim. "Good find, Cokie, that was tricky." She stared at me for a few moments, then moved the game to the side of the house near the daffodil shoots. After another leaf pile and two mud rut hides, she lay down in the front yard, contentedly gnawing on the bone.

As the sun's last rays shone through the trees, the stillness of the evening setting in, I began to understand the greater meaning of Cocoa's game. We had played it before, but never like today. The whole time she was alert, focused on a clear mission, determined on it being with me. It was as if she ignored all the changes in her body and she was well again. She was light again. I felt a wave of love and gratitude for her, for the enormous gift she had given me.

Very little snow remained in the yard, one area being in the shade of the spruce tree by the big rock. Cocoa purposefully went there to rest on the dwindling mass. I took pictures of her, wanting to forever ingrain her in my memory. She raised her head as if intentionally posing, then let her gaze fall deep into the woods.

After having a cup of tea inside, I returned to find her noisily knocking the marrow bone against her teeth. She paused as something moved up the path. I concentrated on her eyes, briefly locking with mine, acknowledging a deeper connection. The afternoon sun gleamed in the background, radiating a halo of light directly on Cocoa. I framed her face with my hands. "I love you, Cokie." I felt her response ever so gently in my heart.

My mind raced to think of all the places Cocoa loved, where we could bring her happiness through familiarity. We helped her into the car and opened the windows so she could relish in the coolness of the ride. She observed the road ahead, her front paws briefly resting on the center console until she resorted to the comfort of the back seat. She stuck her nose out to face the wind. "Where are we going, Cokie?" Her softly tufted ears perked up, and she looked at me with interest. "On an adventure!" I clapped my hands enthusiastically.

We didn't get very far on the dirt road before the ruts appeared. Mud season had begun. The tires eased along the wet tracks, but soon they increased in number and depth. Mama slowed the car to a crawl while navigating through them. "You can do it!" I said. There was no turning back now. We rounded a bend in the road and some utility trucks forced us to the right side, luckily not too close to the gutter rut that would have inevitably pulled us in. Cocoa growled at some workmen as we passed by.

In direct visibility was the road to Hopkins Pond. The ruts diminished, but the pot holes and puddles still made the ride slow. Cocoa tilted her head into the bountiful scents until we arrived. A sign caught our attention from the New Hampshire Fish and Game Department. "WARNING! Abundance of water snakes in pond." I didn't know much about them aside from the ones Matt had seen swimming in the Coral Sea. Those were extremely dangerous. Cocoa seemed to understand the circumstance as she made no move toward the pond and headed onto the winding trail of the perimeter.

I remembered the times Cocoa and I had walked through the woods, down past Elbow Pond, and on the paths that led to the road here. We went along this same trail, full of jutting tree roots, mossy rocks, and many forms of scat. A less-frequented place by humans, it was noticeably popular with wildlife.

Cocoa discovered something at the base of a large tree. "It's too muddy! Let's go back," Mama called from behind me. She was right. "Where's Cocoa?"

"She's just around the corner," I said. "What is it, girl?" She glanced up, distracted from her find, her nose covered in mud and pine needles. She was so alert with her dominating senses, I didn't want to take her away from this. I didn't know if we'd ever return.

Driving uphill in the opposite direction of the terrible ruts, we passed the old cemetery on the slope, the white house that used to be a camp, and down the hill by the haunted-looking cabins. Upon reaching the new bridge across another network of brook leading to Elbow Pond, a gas truck hogged the road and charged by us, oblivious to the imminent mud.

At the boulder barrier to Mountain Brook, Cocoa vigorously sniffed up to the top of the hill. With the brook only a stone's throw away, she stopped abruptly and stared at the water.

There was a distinct pause as if she was in deep contemplation before decidedly turning back toward the car.

One more stop — Highland Lake. This was where I had taken Cocoa as a puppy who loved every minute of digging in the sand and bravely jumping after the little waves. She was fearless, and everything was exciting to her. The following summer, we went swimming, and she herded me from the depths. The sun had been low in the sky, much like it was now.

Despite the "No Dogs" sign, we continued. Cocoa portrayed her little puppy self again, on a mission to the beach, pausing to decipher scents along the way. She cautiously approached a bob house at the shoreline and peered inside. Perhaps it was a whiff of fish that tempted her to investigate until something within fell and sent her jumping back.

Thin sheets of ice floated on the water's surface, and Cocoa waded into the gap between them. She dipped her nose to blow bubbles and raised her head, her coat voluminous with her proud stance. Her gaze was somewhere in the distance. A long stream of water drizzled from her chin, almost frozen in time, and she looked as if she was reborn in that moment.

Cocoa stayed in the water for a while, then joined us on the beach to explore the edges of the pond on the other side. Mama knelt to hug her as she peered at my camera. I couldn't capture enough pictures of our treasured companion, for despite her sickness, she was stunningly captivating. All of us walked slower as we left. The remaining ice would soon become one with the lake.

⸺

We set up the chairs and table outside, positioned toward the afternoon sun. Mama put the cookie tray nearby and Cocoa stood there, her tired eyes looking at us, then at the cookies. I picked them apart, put a little piece partially in my mouth, and brought my face close to hers. She accepted the morsel, and I smiled through the tears streaming down my cheeks. When I looked at Mama, she was holding a piece in *her* mouth, offering it to Cocoa, who without hesitation, took it ever so gently.

Katie and Ben drove into the yard. I saw their sorrowful reactions as they greeted Cocoa. They couldn't stay long but had solo visits outside with her, trying to cope with the challenge of saying goodbye. With the sound of the vehicle doors closing, I caught Cocoa's brief awareness as she turned to watch them leave. The painful realization of this finality struck me hard, and my throat ached with the tremendous emotion piling up from my heart.

I just wanted to erase her pain. Her agony. I had accepted the decision we were faced with, not absorbing the reality we would encounter afterward. My mind *couldn't* and wouldn't go there. Perhaps it was a barricade to protect myself, to protect Cocoa from further anguish and help free her. I was determined to be part of every step, blessed to be by her side no matter how much it broke me to watch her slip away. Despite my efforts to heal her, she was riddled with disease, her life becoming less recognizable. She was telling us enough. It was time.

The vet wasn't answering our calls. The night carried on. Hour by hour seemed to drag as we went outside and back in, Cocoa's vision, her focus so far removed. We arranged couch cushions, bedding, and pillows around her, trying to make her comfortable but to no avail. She couldn't stop moving, approaching the threshold of all-consuming exhaustion. Gratefully, I had the strength and endurance to stay with her.

The faint light of dawn crept through the trees, and we had reached the fateful point. Painfully. Finally. The phone rang, and it was the vet. *One more hour.* Cocoa paced under the kitchen table, and I quickly called Barb to give her the chance to see her. Cocoa's tail bud wiggled slightly when our friend came to say goodbye.

As Mama reclined the car seats, I saw her strained expression. She held such fortitude but would ultimately have to release an enormity of emotion. We lifted Cocoa into the back space, but even with her struggle to breathe, she climbed onto the passenger seat. I squeezed in next to her, and she collapsed on my lap.

Every moment, every minute of that drive was lived in the present. The sun brightly announced the day, reminding me that regardless of the scale of events, the world around us would continue. Down the road and a glance toward Barb's house with Suka inside, unaware that he wouldn't see his friend again.

We stopped to help Cocoa reposition herself. She was the calmest she had been since the morning before the violent escalation of her sickness. Time was an illusion. It was forever, yet it was short-lived. We were one, going into this together, and unbeknownst to me, we would leave together as Cocoa's heart would be eternally felt.

I propped Mr. Froggy onto my knee, and putting on a brave disposition, I began what had become our story — *The Little Mouse, The Red Ripe Strawberry, and the Big Hungry Bear*. Unexpectedly, my voice had strength in it, support from something invisible to my eyes. It was my intention to deliver this exactly as I always had, so Cocoa and I could share it one last time.

I heard the words and intonations as if I was listening to another person, feeling the gravity of each utterance, of every movement. Midway through reading, I saw we were already at Webster Lake, only ten minutes longer. Cocoa was sitting quietly, listening with a sort of innocence. The sun beckoned to us with growing warmth as if trying to offer some comfort… And there we were. Parked. Silent with emotion. I kissed Cocoa's head and opened the door. She climbed down knowingly, composed yet her mouth agape with distress. It was truly time.

She circled the room before being lifted up on the table, the vets beside her, while Mama and I stood witnessing what didn't seem real. The world ceased to exist when Cocoa looked directly at me with purpose I could feel throughout my entire being. Her eyes communicated an understanding, a connection far beyond words. She was somehow completely collected in what was happening, her body suddenly at ease, and I knew she was ready. She was okay, and she wanted me to know that.

Her last exhale and sigh, and in one graceful motion, she walked her front paws forward and slid her chin to rest on them for the final time, her gaze falling still. She was perfect and so beautifully at peace. My heart burst with relief and sheer devastation as I clung onto my best friend and buried my weeping face into her lovely brown coat.

The vet had wrapped Cocoa's bottom half in a bag, the strong smell indicated why, and her body was placed in the back of Mama's car. I felt numb. I lay alongside her, stroking her silky cheek as I looked at her frozen stare. There was complete silence during the ride home, my sobs stifled by Cocoa's mane. When the car engine stopped, I couldn't move. Wholly depleted of energy, I drifted off to sleep only to be awoken by a flock of turkeys as they took flight over the car. For a brief moment, I believed Cocoa was alive again.

Anger filled me when I peered through my foggy glasses at the black bag encasing her as if she was to be casually discarded in the weekly dump run. The thought was appalling. Mama returned to the car with a bucket of soapy water and some cloths, and we removed the bag and lovingly washed Cocoa. Her body had lost its warmth aside from where my head had been on her chest. Finally, we cut a piece of her smooth undercoat to remember her by. The idea of taking anything more felt like a sacrilege.

"James said he'd be here midday to help us bury her," Mama said quietly. Soon he drove into the yard and unloaded some digging tools. I was so grateful to him as I knew how little strength Mama and I had left. Parting from Cocoa's body, I went inside to wash my grief-stricken face, encompassed by a deep, aching emptiness.

The rest of the day went by in slow motion. James discovered a burial site that was so fitting, it seemed destined. It was to the left of the back paths that Cocoa and I used to run together, on higher ground amongst some deciduous trees and a few towering pines. It so happened that this was the first area where she had hidden her prized bone for me only days earlier, as if she intended for that spot to be designated for something meaningful. It was around where I used to get kindling with her… And it was right by where my father used to sit and whistle to the birds. Fully visible from the kitchen window, the last sunrays would fall there before disappearing for the night.

James dug and dug, never once complaining. He gave us the space to kiss Cocoa goodbye, then he gently wrapped her in the soft red blanket she had chewed holes in years ago. "And Mr. Froggy," I said, choked up as I handed him the little toy Cocoa had so adored. He placed her in the depth of the dug earth, delicately folding the corner of the blanket over her face. We stood in silence.

"If anyone wants to say anything or sing…" he suggested. I paused through sniffles.

"Thank you for being my best friend, Cokie," I said.

So emotionally drained, Mama and I watched as James shoveled dirt, gradually covering up our beloved Cocoa's body. When her grave was filled in, my brother carefully took the topsoil he had set aside and replaced it before spreading leaves across the terrain. "That will all grow back nicely," he told us, "and will deter any animals from digging."

He proceeded to design the space, inlaying a heavy piece of granite to mark the entrance of Cocoa's garden. The small saplings around it would be nourished as she became one with the earth. It was an honorable place of rest, known by human and canine alike as I remembered Suka lying on the grave not long after, leaning on his paws in silent grieving.

Mixed precipitation started as snow that blanketed the land anew, followed by drizzle that coated the snow. The temperature reached freezing point. Now, ice-covered branches were frozen in a glass-like delicacy — the short pine needles portrayed crystalline forms magical in their appearance, while the long pine needles drooped downward in motionless entrapment. The tree boughs were so heavy from the new frost, they resembled giants held back in time, unable to lift their encrusted limbs. It was a contrasting combination of beauty and mourning, enlightenment and numbness.

CHAPTER TWELVE:

Always

I had a dream so vivid, I could remember every aspect of it on that early morning after Cocoa's death. My face was stained with tears through my recollections.

I heard the floorboards creak and reached my hand over the edge of the bed to feel a warm lick on my palm. Right away, I knew it was Cocoa. I slid onto the floor and she was there looking at me, the two of us utterly ecstatic in our reunion. I threw my arms around her, crying that I love and miss her so much. A tear hit my arm, hers mixed with mine. She whimpered while I sobbed. Time was of no essence. I had the distinct feeling of holding her in a tight embrace, her eyes gazing into mine, conveying an emotional depth incomprehensible to describe. I smoothed her silky coat and felt relief, happiness, and love. Then I knew she needed to go and she turned into Holly. I continued to hold her until she started to slip away. Her hair became coarse, and she now had a bushy tail. I realized I was touching Suka's back as I watched him/her leave and heard footsteps descending the stairs.

I awoke to hear soft pattering down the outside staircase.

As dusk settled in, I could hear the nocturnal creatures becoming active. The tiniest thing could deceive with seeming loudness that broke the stillness of the dark. I rested my chin on the windowsill, peering out from my front row seat to the nightly entertainment I preferred. This time, though, without my precious companion who had loved to do this as much as me. I turned to the right and could just discern the glint of her eye, her watchful stare, her poised grace. I went to brush her velveteen cheek, and for a whisper of a moment, I felt it. Then my rational mind kicked in, and I was a lone watchman once again.

She had been by the spruce tree my parents planted decades ago. She had been at the top of the well road near the cabin, patiently guarding the landscape. She had been by the woodpile, cooling herself on the damp ground. She had been by the raspberry bushes, in the front yard, upon the top landing of the outside staircase with her front paws bent over the edge… Her scent had dissipated. The brown fluff that she once shed was no longer in the leaves or in the corners of rooms. The wild animals crept closer and closer to the house.

Walking to the pond alone, I hung my head low, the pine needles leading me along a path that went on forever. My ears blocked out sounds, my eyes refused to look where the pine cones could be found in abundance, my heart shattered as I made my way through the tall pines that now seemingly haunted the hilltop. The pond was stagnant, the boathouse floor was littered with smithereens of organic matter, rocks sat waiting, acorns left discarded. Her mark was everywhere, yet she wasn't visible to me anymore — a ghost of a memory.

It was as if I hardened with the realization that she was gone. A part of me fractured and departed from my body as

Cocoa had from hers. I had to accept what pained me to admit, but instead I let my walls go up and buried my grief in a secret vault deep within.

⇀

Cocoa's yellow eyes intently communicated her warm spirit. She stood staring from a distance. Now I was hugging a big dog, her identity unmistakable, and I couldn't let go.

⇀

Suka accompanied me on a walk to the field, exploring the various scents in the woods that distracted him from the open road. I was quiet. Only days ago, I was here with Cocoa, taking in the usual scenery at a slowed pace. Now, as we approached the field on the left, I looked at the overgrown animal path.

With the subtlety of an apparition, two fawns stood almost camouflaged in the dried grass, innocently observing me, their white spots indicating their tender age. I caught myself gasp. I had never seen fawns before, and here they were, allowing me to take in their beautiful presence. After what seemed like minutes of being locked in this gaze, Suka barked, and fleetingly, they disappeared.

I wandered down by the well house later, barely catching sight of a doe leaping off toward the fields in the distance. I started to understand the significance of deer in my life. The doe at Lady's grave, the one at the garden right after Paw's passing, and today, the fawns and quite possibly their mother, so close to Cocoa's death. The message was clear to me that they were animal totems of mine, showing me the transition, grace, and renewal of life — that it never really ends, it just cycles on. Hope would exist indefinitely.

⇀

I knew I had to do it. I *needed* to. To connect with Cocoa and keep her memory alive. The lack of sound during the drive to the mountain was strangely deafening, the silence as loud as her excited barks. I imagined her paws on the center console as she watched the road ahead, eagerly announcing our whereabouts. She licked my face in appreciation and then faded into the background.

"Here we go, Cokie!" I said through a choked-up voice, trying to convince myself otherwise. We— I arrived at the parking lot and got out. All was quiet. But as I neared the beginning of the trail we always took, I knew I wasn't alone. I pushed onward, all the while surrounded by a strong presence.

I stopped at the meditation rock for a drink of water. The trees creaked familiarly, the chilly mountain air dried my sweat. The rocks, the exposed tree roots, the melting ice. Everything was there as I remembered it, and somehow, so was Cocoa. The open pine forest felt protected, and I could hear whispers in the wind.

It wasn't about getting to the top of the mountain, it was about every step I was taking to feel, grieve, and ultimately heal. The sky was dismally overcast and the wind blew strong as if dissuading me from lingering at the summit. Still, I navigated to Cocoa and my spot and made a dedication to her, then bypassed our list of hikes carved on the metal wall to begin the descent.

I picked up my pace, moving along the frosty ground. The emotion that I thought I had locked away, almost frozen until now, suddenly broke its ice as heavy tears ran down my face like droplets of blood. My vision blurred. I sniffed and persisted on, approaching the end of the rocky path, and stopped to take out a tissue to wipe my nose.

As I lifted my gaze, I was drawn to the white birch tree directly opposite me. My heart flooded with exhilarating love as I saw what was, with no doubt in my mind, a sign from Cocoa! Carved in the tree was a heart with **A + C†** inscribed in it, and beside it was **4 ever**. I was amazed. Despite the lack of her physical presence, she was so obviously with me in a form difficult to comprehend. I was yearning to feel her love again, and she had given me another immense gift. A piece of undeniable proof of her continued existence. Cocoa was with me forevermore.

The dreams were constant, and in the early morning hours, I recorded them.

I had a rod and was putting it in the edge of Cocoa's grave, pushing into the earth to dig her up, careful not to go near where her head rested. Then I was lying on the floor with her after she had been euthanized. I just kept staring at her face, stroking her soft coat. I did this for a long time until all of a sudden, her eyes opened and she got up! She was skinny and hungry, and I searched the house to find some dog food.

A white wolf-looking puppy appeared and circled me, wanting food too. I got enough for both dogs, and when I saw Cocoa again, she was her small, fuzzy puppy self! I fed them and gave Cocoa extra because the euthanizing dose had made her really hungry after it had eaten the cancer from her body. Now she was hopping all over the place, this bundle of love, as Mama watched in disbelief.

Cocoa continued to play outside as more family visited, and I could feel everyone's joy. She wiggled delightfully, licked my face, and rolled onto her back for a tummy rub. A big box caught my attention as it blew off the kitchen counter and onto the floor. Inside was a tiny puppy! I felt comforted by this newfound gift.

What did all of this mean? Was it the answer to helping me grieve? A sign that Cocoa would be reborn?

I finally sat at the piano I had been avoiding. I played a chord and stopped. Another. I waited. Somewhere far away, I thought I could hear a whimper, perhaps a drawn-out note. I played more, and as the sounds evolved, I found the words to describe my pain and wrote a song. *"Oh, I'm lost, without you here, wholeheartedly..."* I felt my voice weaken as I burst into tears.

⁊

Looking at the most recent pictures of Cocoa, they were of exceptional quality, and I was overcome with emotion as I zoomed in on every detail. Then, in the collections taken throughout the years, it was gripping to see how this single being had made such an enormous impact on me. Her image needed to be kept alive, memorialized on canvas.

Mama and I ordered several prints, and I chose two for myself. One where she was standing in the pond — the strands from her coat merged with the pine needles that had collected on the surface of the water, her yellow eyes wise and loving. So much was captured in that moment. The other picture was of her sitting in a pickup truck. Her gaze seemed to stare into my soul, energetic and familiar, and again, an indescribable "knowing" in her eyes. It was incredible how in those two pictures, her life was eternal.

⁊

Cocoa's presence was still so strong, it was perplexing not to see her form. This afternoon felt no different. Mama and I picked up Suka to venture to Mountain Brook. As soon as we started on the trail, flashbacks of Cocoa blowing bubbles filled my mind. The sun happily shone, the birds chirped as they welcomed the spring weather, and Suka disappeared into the woods ahead of us.

We paused briefly to look at the water that diverged in the distance, a changed course previously unnoticed. "The

Road Not Taken" echoed in my thoughts. The thawing ground became muddy in spots, while pockets of shade held ice-glazed puddles and powdery snow rested on leaves. Branches cracked and rocks tumbled before Suka joined us in the area that Cocoa had always been nervous about.

The dark and damp coolness of the big trees and boulders brought on that recognizable feeling of being watched. Rounding the bend to where the brook was accessible again, Suka bolted across the terrain and leapt into the water and back out, his soaking body wildly circling us. Mama and I smiled in acknowledgment, knowing Cocoa was there running alongside her friend.

"What is that?" I motioned up the hill at something red hanging from a tree. We approached it. Randomly draped yet almost precisely placed was a fleece blanket. The sun shone on the corner, and I reached out to spread it. A few jagged holes were in the fabric, looking very much like bite marks, and one was in the distinct shape of a heart. We stared in awe as the light cast its pattern against the tree, and silently, we both knew. Mama had received *her* sign.

I was clearing the paths of kindling, stockpiling it for the stoves that continued to warm the house through the chilly nights. As I picked up some branches from part of a fallen tree, I heard tapping on a window and spotted Mama waving at me. I smiled and waved back before carrying the brimming box to the front door. She opened it for me. "Come and see," she said, pointing out the window. No further explanation was needed as my eyes focused on exactly what she saw.

It was the fallen tree, but it wasn't. It looked exactly like Cocoa lying there, her gaze up the path ahead as if waiting for her canine friend to appear. I felt a tear roll down my cheek. It was astonishing that from an angle, our minds were tricked by this illusion, our hearts suddenly restored with the feeling that Cocoa was physically there once again. How a simple change in perspective could bring us such comfort and enlightenment.

Despite the many reassuring signs from Cocoa, I remained so broken by her death. I quietly packed for my return to Australia. This used to be the ultimate heart-wrenching moment of saying goodbye as she rested her chin on her paws, looking at me with sad eyes. But it was inconceivably harder this time as I sat beside her grave.

"Cokie, I know you are all around now, but I just wish I could hug you again, I miss you so…" The tears flowed down my face uncontrollably. It was as if I was leaving her forever. There would never be another heartfelt welcome of hers to come home to — her bum wiggling vigorously, her whimpering, her "love" eyes, and the feeling of my being her most treasured gift.

I kept one of Cocoa's old marrow bones. It soothed me to hold it close as I recalled how much time she spent with it, smoothing the edges as I read to her, throwing it down the stairs, burying it for me to find. It was like a pacifier, a teddy bear, a cherished, sentimental reminder. I discovered that Mama, too, had found the same consolation.

I drive along, haunted by your absence, my heart aches. I find myself singing that I am not alone with you close by and am reassured. Although a witness to your physical demise, your excited bark still rings around me. I feel your body brush past, then you've jumped up on my bed, circling into your resting spot. I can just hear inhalations and exhalations, a faint snore even, and I know you have not left my side.

I still can't believe it. I don't want to believe it. This was the first trip home where my beloved friend would not greet me, and I felt a powerful sense of emptiness already. A dark and gaping hole that was the anticipated absence of love from Cocoa. Such a monumental part of my life in the woods — gone.

Over three months ago was that final day, yet it seemed like forever. The pain pierced my heart. Guided by this wave of emotion, I put pen to paper through automatic writing.

"I am there with you, by your side. I am there, waiting for your return. You can still feel my licks upon your face, my hugs, my love for you. I am there, Mandy. Always."

A plump tear rolled down my cheek as I was once again consoled by this invisible source.

Climbing the hill along the same forest and road circuit we used to walk, my heart sank to see the massive clearing of trees, making the area almost foreign to me. The familiarity of the densely-wooded landscape was wiped from my memory. But continuing on, an insightful revelation was uncovered. The clarity that somehow helped heal these fresh wounds. The perspective *had* changed with the destructive clear-cutting, all of those precious trees fallen, but everything was open, lighter, and the once-obscured view now drew attention to the pond where so many of our wondrous adventures took place.

As I stepped back, the picture became even clearer, and a feeling of utter completeness washed over me. I saw how happy, free, and protected I had been with my beautiful companion. It was like we were in our own world, experiencing new horizons, taking in the beauty of nature in a language that was almost entirely nonverbal. I was "home" in my heart when I was in Cocoa's company, as if we had known each other far longer than this lifetime. We were of the same spirit. With her connection and unconditional love, I was supported to blossom in profound ways.

Waking with complete recall of my dreams was not by chance.

Cocoa was her excited, playful self. She was beaming, and I could hear her happy bark. She came over to be hugged by us, her presence strong. It was amazing to feel such comfort. The scene changed, and I broke down at the sight of Mama sitting there alone. I told her I just wasn't ready to accept that Cocoa was gone, and I don't think I ever will.

And I don't have to. She was still very much a part of my life — amidst my dreams, then the source of my inspiration during waking hours, communicating through nature and automatic writing. Signs from her were always appearing, making me stronger with their meaning.

Reading late into the night, I paused to look where Cocoa used to lay with me, chewing on her bone as I read to her, and felt a pang of sadness. At that very instant, my phone indicated a new email and I reached over to check it. The subject line was "Find your spirit guides."

Saying goodbye to Cocoa was saying goodbye to my best friend who represented so much more to me than I ever truly realized when she was alive. She separated me from the worry, fear, and responsibility I wasn't ready for. She was always by my side in the woods that engulfed us with sensory meditation, focusing on being present, living within the moment. Listening into the depths of the pines to the water that trickled along the earth, to hear the first call of a new life, the whistle of wind through the maze of creation…

She brought me to this place of ultimate freedom and peace where I looked past my physical limitations into the rays that highlighted what seemed lesser, forgotten. She helped me reconnect with nature, taking me from the suburban life I had made so far away and my memory of any constraints I encountered. She reminded me of what made me feel alive, drawing me out of the numbness that had slowly seeped into my being as mundane routine. We were together in those times of grateful appreciation, in vast imagination.

Cocoa was instrumental in my further spiritual explorations. Facing her sickness and the all-encompassing factors it brought, I was guided to alternative modes of healing, and in those last few weeks of her life, I do believe they helped. I literally *felt* the energy coursing through my body to hers. It was in that light, that awareness, when I was inspired. My love for her, our bond — Cocoa led me there.

I found my way to her in the spirit world through a shamanic journey. My intention was to locate and reunite with her, and ultimately to derive comfort and healing in doing so. The drum beats on…

The ancient tree with holes in it is where I discovered my animal guide Athena, a white-tailed doe. She nuzzles my face, then we descend a long flight of stairs, going into the darkness below the tree. It is cool in temperature and there is daylight ahead. A large greenscape with rolling hills awaits us in the spirit world, and I hear Cocoa's high-pitched barking in the distance! We go down a slope, and I see her waiting at the shoreline of a pristine little lake. We wade in together like any day, and I get the notion that Lady is there too, somewhere in this land. Cocoa swims around me, herding me. She licks my face and seems really happy. She has abundant energy.

Athena is watching from afar as the sky becomes starry. Cocoa rests by the water at night, and I want to stay with her. I find a hammock between two trees on a little hill overlooking the lake. The moon is out. Cocoa jumps high to join me, and I feel her warm body close. Soon it's time to leave. I tell her of my gratitude and love, then journey back to ordinary reality, thanking Athena before opening my eyes.

My face was wet with tears. Cocoa was safe. She was happy. She was *free!*

As I invited my spirit guides into my writing space, Holly walked into the room. She stopped and looked around, seemingly at the invisible energies, then finally made eye contact with me in recognition. And later, as I sat amidst the backyard nature, a magnificent butterfly fluttered near me, catching my eye with her electric blue wings, then disappearing over the fence. In those brief seconds, I was encouraged — *take comfort in that you are never alone.* There are always signs just wanting you to notice them. Always meaning. No coincidences.

It was a divine orchestration that unfolded, as if I was directed to the right scenario, the right beings, the right circumstances for me to grow. Through Cocoa's unfaltering, everlasting love, I saw that our connection continued over distance and time. This nourishing reminder gave me the strength to live so far away. Holly led me to meet Matt, to fall in love. Her independent, energetic nature and companionship was exactly what I needed to keep me active so not to wallow in self-pity. I was blindsided by all I felt I lost when what I gained by having both worlds was so much greater.

The clouds parted as I wrote in my notebook, linked to endless memories. The sun became blinding with its brilliance, a spotlight pointed at me. The consciousness of my work's inspiration reassured me that I was not alone in this writing venture. I opened my heart to Cocoa once more, and by doing this, I found myself channeling her message. She confirmed a lot for me, dissolving the residual emotion I had from leaving her, helping me to understand that we never really parted. As I read to Mama, I could hear her sighing.

"I turned to see she was still following me. She was lost in her mind, and I picked up a pine cone for her to chase me with. She rushed toward me, but I'm fast. I was really fast when I wasn't sick. I was going to the water. I loved it. I wished Mandy would swim with me more like when she would jump off the dock. Those were the good old days. I would go with her to so many places, and I'd always be looking out for her. And sometimes, we would just sit there watching. I loved running with her. The trees were always changing just like life. My family came and went. I was sure lucky to have all of them.

"I knew she'd come back. I could feel her on her way to me. I wanted to see her one last time, but I also knew how emotional it would be. I called to her in the night and she answered. Her heart was broken, and I couldn't leave her. She had to help me go. Mama needed her too. I sat there feeling so different. I was moving out of my body, out of the pain. I felt her warm hands upon me, and it was comforting. It was cold outside, but it was where I could breathe best.

"Everyone came to see me, to say goodbye... but I was only leaving my brown body. My brown body that was full of sickness. I saw her there, her throat stuck, her arms wrapped around my body I looked down upon. I told her in the room. I looked at her to give my message. It was okay. She saved me. They both did. My Mama was so crippled with the pain of loss from Paw too, she could not look at me, but I felt so much love from her. I was sick for a long time, but I needed to stay as long as I did. For Mama. For Mandy to return.

"I loved the woods so much. I choose to stay there often, and sometimes Mama can feel me reach out to her. I am by her side at the table. I see her quietly cry, and I nuzzle at her hand and wait to see if she feels me trying to console her. The sun is low and I remember when we used to walk together. I push to have her do it again, but she doesn't. I want her to know how much I love her, and I see her say goodbye to me. There are times when I speak to her, and she thinks she hears me and she's right. I am there. She is getting better, happier, and she will meet me again, heart to heart.

"And then I hear Mandy call to me, her constant words bringing me to life once again and I am near. It is easier now because I can travel and be there quickly. I see her sitting there writing. I help her, I see her cry. She knows I am there. I knew she needed to go to Australia. But she should know that just because I'm not there for her to hug, she still must return to the woods and know we can still have adventures together. I will protect her always.

"Mandy, you are very special to me. I love you. You are going to be just fine. You are headed in a direction that is so fulfilling, and you are open, which is why I can talk to you like this, in your dreams, and I am around you a lot. Thank you for everything."

When people talk about great love, their one true love in this lifetime, it really stops me in my tracks. I realize that this love is different for me, for it isn't a human who has captured my heart, but a special brown dog with such depth and understanding of the human condition. It only takes a moment of looking into her eyes to recognize something way beyond rational comprehension. Could she have been an angel, a guardian, a guide with a destined purpose?

She has taught me so many core lessons of acceptance, patience, joy, friendship, simplicity, love and courage, along with an overwhelming feeling of grief and loss that has at times felt like I bore an extinguished candle inside me. But now, Cocoa has given me the gift of renewing reminiscence as I relive the wonder-filled life I was so blessed to have had with her as my great love.

With my hand on my heart, I thank her immensely for showing me what unconditional love is. The sliver of light that shone through the door in her final days is now a gateway revealing limitless radiant light. *And the journey lived has become the journey just begun.*

Afterword

Just as the fallen leaves become part of the earth, everything changes form. *Changes form.* I have not truly lost Cocoa. She will always be there in my life, simply in different ways. The heartfelt journey I shared with her moved me so deeply that I was compelled to write about it, unveiling astounding insight. I had found my "more."

It wasn't something physically tangible or anything I would find through an outward reach. It had been inside of me all along, and even though I had recognized it, known it on some level, it hadn't seemed enough to me so I kept searching. I thought it would be like fireworks going off — a spectacle of such magnitude that I couldn't miss it — when it was actually quite the opposite.

It had inherently revealed itself, and a tremendous peace swept over me as the "more" filled me with the most immeasurable feeling. It was where I found myself most often with Cocoa. She led me to self-discovery in those quiet instances of presence, pure existence without expectation, utterly experiencing the moment. And in that calmness, that serenity, I understood what I had been looking for this entire time. *The blissful state of my very being.*

No matter what, I am going to be okay. I know that it is amidst the greatest challenges where I will learn, grow, and expand into new understanding. The answers lie within, and because of that, they're infinite, eternal, always. Magic and adventure are everywhere. It doesn't matter who or how old you are, where you live… If you can only stop, close your eyes and take a deep breath, you will see the colors show themselves.

I am strong and know it's time. Time to let go. Letting go doesn't mean that the love and memories aren't held sacred, they will be forever cherished. What it means is I can release the emotional crippling that prevents me from seeing the light Cocoa's life has brought to mine. It is with a newfound clarity that I can move on with so much *more* because of her. I smile as I feel her close in my heart, and again, she is by my side — my guardian, my angel, *I celebrate you, dear Cocoa!*